The Inside Truth About Organized Crime

by BISHOP

Elevate Entertainment
Franklin, TN 37067

Both Sides of the Fence

Both Sides of the Fence
© 2013 by BISHOP
ISBN: 978-0-9911199-0-5
www.BishopOutreach.com

Published and printed by:
Elevate Entertainment and Bishop Outreach

Distribution by:
Elevate Entertainment • Franklin, TN 37067
(615) 595-4216 • (615) 293-3919

Cover Design: Tracy Lesch

Printed in the United States of America

18 17 16 15 14 13   1 2 3 4 5

Both Sides of the Fence

DEDICATION

"To my wife and best friend. You have taught me that I can do all things through Christ. I don't have to be anyone but me and you have restored family in my life and I love you for that. You and Lou mean the world to me. Thank you for just being you."

Both Sides of the Fence

ACKNOWLEDGMENT

Because of our current situation, I can't publicly acknowledge or thank everyone involved. But you know who you are, and I'm eternally grateful for your love and support.

Both Sides of the Fence

TABLE OF CONTENTS

Both Sides of the Fence

"See what great love the Father has lavished on us, that we should be called children of God! And that is what we are! The reason the world does not know us is that it did not know him.

Dear friends, now we are children of God, and what we will be has not yet been made known. But we know that when Christ appears, we shall be like him, for we shall see him as he is."

1 John 3:1-2

Chapter 1

Beginning of the End

I roared through the open gate of the wooden fence that surrounded the Forsaken Ones Motorcycle Club property. With the gritty tunes of Jamie Johnson blaring from my speakers, I backed my Harley Road Glide into its usual spot. The sweet aroma of tonight's dinner hung heavy on the dusty, still air. I grinned. My favorite: chicken, tamales, and refried beans. In one swift motion, I slipped off the bike like I had thousands of times since becoming the leader three years ago.

Tired from a six-hour round trip ride to Lake Havasu to take care of business, I wanted nothing more than to grab a quick bite and settle in for a relaxing evening with my wife. Midway between my bike and the front door, two patched brothers and a probate pulled up beside me. None looked happy.

"Boss," one of them yelled before shutting off his bike. "We need to talk."

Still in stride, I called over my shoulder, "Walk and talk."

The trio followed me into the clubhouse; through the living room where three other brothers sat on the couch, one with his girl on his lap;

past the bar on the left; and into the patch holder's room in the back. I touched the American flag that hangs over the entrance and said, "God Bless America," a habit I developed the day we opened this house. Inside, I looked at Tuna, the probate, and said, "You know you can't be in here. Now get out." I waved him back toward the main part of the club. Without a word, he left, and I closed the door behind him. To Chief, a pot-bellied man with a long ponytail who demanded the conversation, I said, "What's up?"

"There's a Fed in the house."

I snickered. "I doubt that."

The other brother, Goat, a loyal but quick-tempered original member, chimed in. "Why would we lie to you?"

"Where did you hear this?" I countered.

"Gene from the Phoenix house said he saw a letter."

I plopped onto the tattered leather couch next to the door. "A letter from who?"

"Paul."

I laughed. "He's a probate. There's no way he'd have seen a letter like that." While Goat stammered to say something, I asked, "Why would someone show him the letter?"

"I didn't ask." Goat said. "All I know is he sent me a text saying we have a Fed in the house."

"What else did he say?"

"Nothing."

14

"Let me see the text."

Goat pulled a beat up Smartphone from inside his leather vest, tapped a few buttons, and handed the phone to me.

"What the hell? Do you chew on this thing?"

"Funny."

"Looks like you do."

"Those are from my dog."

After wiping the phone on my jeans, I glanced at the text. "He's joking," I said, tossing the phone back to Goat.

"How do you know that?"

"Look at the messages above it." I arched a brow. "He's messing with you. So why would he all of a sudden get serious?"

Chief answered instead, "I don't think he's joking."

"Well, boys, I think he is. No way we have a Fed in the house." I stood and opened the door. "Now, let's eat."

I scanned the room for my wife, Sissy. As usual, she was busy in the kitchen. I watched her hand a dinner plate to a drunken Pippie, a property girl who couldn't keep her hands off any of the men and was the girlfriend of Badger. I shook my head, wondering how someone so little could drink so much and how Badger could tolerate a promiscuous girlfriend. After giving Sissy a quick kiss, I said in a hushed tone, "Someone thinks we have a Fed in the house."

Fear replaced the normal sparkle in her eyes. "How?"

My lips still near her ear, I said, "Don't worry. I convinced them it's not true."

She whirled to face me. "And they believed you?"

"Of course." I smiled. "I've gotten pretty good at living on both sides of the fence."

After dinner Sissy and I sat in rockers on the side of the porch. We faced the western horizon with the Harquahala Mountains in the distance. Whenever in town, we loved to watch the evening sky blaze with breathtaking hues of burnt orange, pink, purple and red before each gave way to a sky filled with twinkling stars.

"I think this is my favorite time of the day," said Sissy, snuggling against my left arm.

I kissed the top of her head. "Mine too."

Life here outside of Wittmann was much different than Phoenix, although we're only thirty-five miles northwest. More laid back. Less stress than living and riding in a big city. But the widening of Highway 60 about a year ago brought more tourists to town than we cared to have. But they loved our popular watering holes—El Besar and Los Gatos.

Several minutes of silence slipped by before Sissy spoke again. "What are we gonna do if they find out?"

"Find out what?" Her question pulled me from admiring what looked like a master's touch of a thin purple line around a vibrant red cloud.

"You know what." She squeezed my arm.

"There's nothing to worry about." I ran my hand through her soft, black hair. "I told you, I took care of it."

The sun eased below the mountaintop. I took a deep breath and held it. What an evening, I thought. How in the heck did someone find out? And the questions at dinner. "If it's true, do we kill that guy?" "How do we kill the guy?" I can't believe Willy, my vice president, said to castrate the guy and make him eat his balls. I knew Willy was a little off, but not *that* much. After a while, I had to tell the guys to shut up, that I'd heard enough. "If there was a Fed in the house, don't you think I'd know about it?" That got 'em to shut up for the rest of the meal. But I didn't know how long it might be before someone brought it up again. Most of the guys couldn't keep their mouth shut when they drank, so the questions would resurface. And probably soon. Like later tonight.

Sissy snuggled me again. "I love you."

Eyes fixed on the darkening horizon, I whispered back, "I love you too."

"I'll be glad when this is over."

"Me too. I wish Red would give us an end date. This is—"

Boots clicking on the wooden porch cut our conversation short. A probate rounded the corner and stopped when he saw us. "Sorry."

Before Sissy or I could reply, what sounded like a half-dozen bikes roared into the compound. While not uncommon to hear bikes this time of the night, we weren't expecting guests. I jumped to my feet and said to her, "Stay here." To the probate that had interrupted our quiet time, I yelled, "Check the gate."

"I'm not sitting out here alone." Sissy was on her feet. "I'm going with you."

We rounded the corner together. I guided her toward the front door. "Go inside."

I glanced toward the parking area. Seven patched brothers from another house climbed off their bikes while two white support vans— with two probates each—idled nearby. My stomach churned.

Jumping off his bike, Music Man, a Phoenix charter member, said, "I was hoping you were here."

I stepped off the porch and shook his hand. "Where else would I be?" I tried to read his face, but dusk and sunglasses concealed his reason for the unannounced visit.

"What brings you out of the city? Drink all the coffee at the Phoenix house?"

He laughed and looked at Phil, another Phoenix charter member. "We need to talk."

Phil shouted to the guys in the support vans, "Probates get on the gate. No one comes in and no one sure as hell goes out."

I headed inside, motioning for all to follow. "Okay, boys. C'mon on in and let's talk."

"Round your boys up and let's go into the back room."

Inside, I ordered all the patched members into the patch holder's room. Goat and Tuna exchanged a glance and rose from one of the three couches in the living room. Five others abandoned either the comforts of a couch or their spot at the bar. "I'll be right back, baby," one of the guys at the bar said to his girl. "I'm sure it's nothing."

As I walked by the edge of the bar I noticed a wide-eyed Sissy in the corner giving me a "what the hell?" look. I pushed a slow-moving member in front of me. "Are you walking in molasses?"

The seven Phoenix members stood outside the room until we entered first. This wasn't normal procedure. Guests were supposed to enter first. Instead of arguing the point, I followed my boys in. I reached up to touch the flag but one of the visitors smacked my hand away. Without looking back and reaching up for a second time, I said, "Don't do that again." This time they allowed this important-to-me, but-strange-to-some routine.

Music Man entered, closed the door, and wasted no time getting down to business. "We're here to shut you down."

"I don't think so," I said, getting in his face. "No one, and I mean no one, comes into my clubhouse," I poked him in the chest for good measure, "and tells me what they're gonna do."

"You don't have a choice," he said, narrowing his eyes behind his sunglasses. "We heard there's a Fed in the house and we're shutting you down and taking your rags."

I threw my hands in the air. "Here we go again with the Fed in the house crap." Cussing, I stomped into the middle of the room. "And what gives you the right to cut off our colors?"

Juvie, a patched brother from a New Mexico chapter, slid a hand into his vest, hesitated, and before he could do anything, Chief pulled on him. Juvie responded by pulling out a 410 Pistol.

In a move that I'd become accustomed to during my years with the club, each person brandished a pistol, seemingly out of thin air. For a group of people who loved each other as much as we did, it amazed me how much—and how quickly—we could pull on each other. My heart rate didn't even increase anymore when this happened.

"You know damn well that we have the right," Music Man said. "The main house in Phoenix can shut down any house in this state. Do I need to go over all the by-laws with you and your boys?" He returned his gun to its hiding place. The rest of us did the same.

"No, I know the rules." I crossed my arms. "Remember, I helped rewrite them."

"Good," Music Man said. "Now give me your cut."

Pondering the ramifications, I stared at my friend-turned-foe. Then I did the unthinkable. I made a move to take it off.

"Wait." Willy jumped between me and Music Man, and then motioned to Phil. "Come with me."

Willy led Phil into a small bathroom on the opposite side of the room, for what, who knows. While they were gone, I eyed Music Man for a moment. He shrugged. A few minutes later, the two returned. "Boss, we need to talk," Willy said, motioning me into the bathroom. "Step into my office."

Inside, he revealed the deal he made with Phil. We could keep our house open, but we'd have to give up our cuts with rags attached. The Phoenix house would keep them until the Fed issue got sorted out.

Sounded like a fair solution to me. "Why'd you broker the deal with him?" I asked.

Willy looked me dead in the eye. "Because we have been to hell and back together and it won't end like this."

Chapter 2

A New Beginning

I wasn't a lifelong biker like some of the guys in the club, but I wasn't a saint either. That's why the Feds came to me for an undercover assignment in a motorcycle club. Because of my background, and my history for living outside the law, I was able to fit into the organization rather easily.

The day I got out of prison, I vowed to change my life. I'm not the first person to make that promise. And I certainly won't be the last. I never expected my life to move in the directions that it did. At times, I didn't feel like I had a choice. Sometimes we don't. Because of previous transgressions—whether it's lying, stealing, selling drugs, sex trafficking—we don't always get to choose the next steps in our life. Sometimes people with more control, more influence, and more power make those decisions. And you have to move forward under their direction whether you like it or not.

When I got out of jail, I wanted to slip into a small town in Arizona and live peacefully while I put my life back together. I didn't know which town. I thought I might grab a map, close my eyes, and point to a spot. I didn't really care. All I knew was that I wanted nothing to do with the people I hung out with before I went to jail. They weren't the most upstanding people in the community.

We dealt drugs, which was easy because people love drugs. That's why the drug industry brings in more than $65 billion a year in the U.S. We also scammed various businesses around the Phoenix area with an innovative scheme. I don't want to go into detail about that because I don't want to give anyone ideas. One thing we didn't get into was sex trafficking. I don't recall ever having a conversation that we should. Those conversations usually don't take place. It's not like we'd have a meeting and map out a plan for what we wanted to do next, like a board of a directors might do for a Fortune 500 company. For us, word got around about what we were doing. People then would come to us, or we might go to them, and work out a deal to work together. Usually it was a mutually beneficial agreement, done with a handshake, not with pages upon pages of legal documents drawn up by lawyers. We didn't operate that way. A handshake and a man's word was all we needed.

I landed in the state pen because my past caught up to me. It's that simple. In my early twenties I'd been running dope, mostly cocaine, for some guys in southeast Arizona. My partners and me wanted to make some quick cash so we started flipping houses with the drug money.

We'd buy a house, get the money from the bank, and flip it for a buck. Loan officers at the bank were part of the scam as well. Getting the money wasn't a problem. We basically were laundering money. Lots of it. Hundreds of thousands of dollars. The average man would probably choke on the amount of money. To us, it was nothing. Twenty or even fifty dollars to the Joe on Main Street can be a lot of money. That was pennies to us. We dealt with so much money in a day that after a while money was nothing more than a means to the next deal, like trading baseball cards as a kid.

Our scheme worked well until one of my handlers missed a $250,000 payment. To this day, I don't know why he missed the payment. He might have kept the money or he might have been told not to pay. Who knows? Bottom line is he didn't pay me. And it was on.

A hit was put out on me.

Chuck (one of my best buddies) and I had gone camping up in the Tonto National Forest, located near northeast of Phoenix. Elevation over the 2,874,900 acres ranges from 1,300 to 7,900 feet. We wanted to get away to drink beer and smoke pot for a few days and to enjoy nature. The park isn't a dry, barren desert. Campers and parkgoers enjoy a large variety of vegetation and wildlife. Early in the evening of the second day while sipping beer we heard vehicles approaching the camp. My buddy screamed, "Jump in the truck!"

We tore out of there in his 1999 Ford F-150. At first we thought it was bikes, but about six cars, mostly trucks and SUVs, pursued us higher up into the mountain. When we couldn't shake them, I jumped out of the truck when it rounded a corner doing seventy miles an hour. I rolled down the hill to what I thought was safety. Instead, I landed in a bed of fire ants where I had to lay for forty-five minutes. The guys chasing us didn't know exactly where I was so they kept shooting over top of me until it got dark. After the sun set, they gave up and left. When I felt safe, I stripped to my underwear, crawled back up to the road and found my buddy hiding in his truck about a mile back toward camp.

Chuck looked surprised. "What the hell happened to you?"

"Don't ask," I said, still rubbing various parts of my body where I'd been bitten.

"We need to get you out of here or they're gonna kill you."

"You think?"

So we went on the run all over southern Arizona for the next two weeks. We stayed in every little out-of-the-way place you could think of. In that part of the state, there aren't many places. But we found a new place every couple of days.

We drank a lot of beer, chased a few women, smoked more pot and stayed in a roach motel every night. At one place near a town that I can't remember, the roaches were so bad that I watched a group of them push open a cabinet door. At least that's what I thought I saw.

For guys like Chuck and me, it's easy to blend in when you live the lifestyle that we did. Guys who wear three-piece suits couldn't have done what we did. They might think they can. But they really can't.

People like me can blend in better. We know how to treat people with respect, love others, and talk with people. Three-piece guys usually have a pole up their ass and look down on people.

Chuck and I blended in for two weeks before I couldn't take it anymore. Money wasn't an issue. We had more than we needed to stay on the run. Despite living a less-than-honest life, I liked stability. Drinking beer, smoking pot, and staying in a new roach motel every two or three days wasn't the stability I wanted. Or needed. I ended up in Albuquerque, New Mexico.

I bought a bar on the corner of Central Ave SW and Attrisco Drive SW and found a place to stay. The stability I needed was back. I got into my routine of running the bar and operating on little or no sleep. Less than a month after opening the bar, this tired-looking short guy walked in one afternoon around 4:00 and struck up a conversation. Being behind the bar I was used to guys talking. Most wanted me to be their personal psychologist, which no bartender is ever qualified to do. We listen and do our best not to offer advice. Once in a while, though, you get tired of a guy whining and tell him to grow a pair and move on. So on this particular day I'm listening to the whiner go on and on about his marriage and his kids and his job and his in-laws. Normal stuff, until he said, "Do you know Jesse Project?"

I did my best to mask my surprise. I did know Jesse Project. We'd been involved in some dealings before. "Sure, I know him."

He started back on his marriage issue and I half-listened while washing a few glasses. He was midway through a sentence when the phone rang. Glad for the interruption, I said, "Hold that thought," and picked up the phone. I listened to the caller for a minute and hung up. Hoping he'd forgotten his place in the story, I went back to finish wiping off the glasses.

"Was that George Rodriguez?"

I nearly dropped the glass I held in my hand and looked at him. I nodded.

"It seems we're good." He smiled. "Follow me."

He led me outside and walked to a Lexus parked in the lot beside the bar. Concerned now, I took a step back when he popped open the trunk. He pulled out a spare tire and rolled it in my direction. "Welcome home."

Inside was a kilo of coke. I was back in business. For the next three years, I ran the bar and sold dope. I was high on the hog again. And feeling invincible.

Until I received a notice from The Army Reserves that I had to report for duty. When The Reserves call, you must go; it doesn't matter if you own a business or sweep floors for a business. The Reserve provides support for The Army and National Guard and skipping out is not an option. So, I served my country with pride and honor. When I returned I landed in jail because of the warrants out for my arrest.

After doing my time, I set foot into freedom, possibly for the first time in my life, on a bright Monday morning in August 2005. I vowed to make right everything that I could. I knew some past transgressions could not be fixed. Like the time I knuckled up with a guy who wouldn't leave a woman alone as she tried to drink in peace after being dumped by her boyfriend. The guy kept pestering her. When he ignored me for the third time, I took care of business. That landed me in trouble, but I was back to work the next day. Stuff like that I couldn't fix. What I could fix was my inner core. The person at the center of my being. The person that had walked away from God.

So I went back to church.

Convicts often find God in prison. You see it all the time. They come in with a chip on their shoulder. They think they're a badass. They might have shanked (stabbed) someone on the outside so they come in thinking they're gonna run the inside of the prison. They might feel like they got shafted on the outside. Rarely does a guy come in thinking he's in because he deserves it. Each prison was filled with a bunch of guys that "got a bad rap" or "their lawyer didn't do his job." Most are waiting for an appeal that usually doesn't come. There really are only two kinds of prisoners, the ones that have accepted that they are there for their time and those that create hope to deal with the fact that they are not getting out anytime soon. Old-timers often say there are only two ways out: parole or death.

New inmates are in for a rude awakening. Even if they're aware of the gangs, cliques, etc., from watching shows like *Scared Straight* or some fake reality show like that, they have no idea how it really works. Yes, there are gangs in prison. The six major ones are Neta, Aryan Brotherhood, Black Guerilla Family, Mexican Mafia, La Nuestra Familia, and Texas Syndicate. It's a way of life for some of these guys. You rarely see three-piece guys in prison. It happens, but not often. Those guys usually have the money to obtain a good lawyer who can get a reduced sentence, time in a minimum- or low-security prison, or nothing at all.

On the other hand, guys in prison are used to living on the edge of society. But many still come in angry, bitter, and full of themselves. Some try to keep their nose clean. Others join up with a gang right away. To each their own. I joined a gang and quickly moved up the ranks. I spent the next few years fighting, making moonshine, and doing any other thing to survive.

And like I said, some find Jesus. I knew Jesus before I went in, but got pissed off years before, and walked away while waving a middle finger at Him. Now that I was back on the outside, I wanted to find Him, beg for forgiveness, and live His way, not mine. Living my way for years provided me with many wonderful things—lots of booze and drugs, nice cars, and fun-loving friends, more than I can count or care to remember. Of course, to the world and those around me, I had everything a man would or could want. But I got caught and did my time.

Now I had a chance to start over. I first lived in a halfway house and I got help from the Feds to land a job as a line cook at a twenty-four hour diner. I didn't have many friends that I could count on. I didn't have stability yet. But I had two things: desire and motivation.

I didn't want to live the way I had for most of my life. Part of me wanted to live quietly in a house with the proverbial white picket fence, wanted to be well-liked by my neighbors, and to live for God. My cellie in Arizona State Prison tried to get me to services different times, but I didn't want to listen to him, nor his nonsense. A buddy of his, Big Matt, also tried. One day I laid on my bunk trying to read when this guy taps on the bars. "You coming, Boss?"

"I told you three times already, no." I jumped down and got in his face. "Now leave me alone. I don't want to hear about this Jesus crap anymore."

He didn't flinch. "Well, alright. I'll be back tomorrow. Have a blessed day," he said, backing out.

I punched the side of the bunk and stomped out into the yard for a smoke. I don't know what it was, but he got to me. So the next day when he came by, I went with him. Nothing took hold that day like you see on television or read about in a guy's memoir years later. I've heard stories of guys falling out and being overcome by the Holy Spirit. None of that happened that day. To me or anyone else. I don't even recall what Big Matt spoke about that day. It doesn't really matter.

Now on the outside, I was ready. After living years of seeking instant gratification, I wanted the Lord to show me the God that my mom worshipped. One of the godliest women I knew, Mom was always at church whenever the doors were open. She studied her Bible and attended a Bible study every week. I knew I didn't need to clean up; I just needed to go to Him. So I did.

And God had things planned that I never would have dreamed about. Soon after my release, I met a lovely woman named Sissy. I can't say we were complete opposites. We did have some things in common, but our backgrounds were in different zip codes. Literally. While I lived on the fringes of society, she was raised in a rural neighborhood on the outskirts of Phoenix. She went to church, graduated from college, and landed a job selling real estate for Phoenix Real Estate, one of the largest companies in the city. Sweet but sassy, with long black hair, she seemed to be well liked by her co-workers and members of her church, where ironically, we met.

While Sissy and I began our relationship, I went back to church at Calvary Congressional Church in Phoenix. And much to my surprise, church walls didn't collapse when I walked through the doors. I know that never happens, but sinners often feel a church might collapse when they walk through for the first time or return after many years away, particularly if they've done some of the stuff that I did.

Over the years I've been called a go-getter, a doer, a take-charge person. Those characteristics I kept after leaving prison. So, after a few months of attending church, I saw the need for someone to lead the youth. Naturally I stepped up. I approached the senior pastor one Sunday after church.

"Pastor Juan," I said, extending my hand. "When you get a minute, I'd like to chat with you about something."

Shaking my hand, he said, "Would love to, Boss. Give me a few more minutes."

I waited at a high top in back of the church's coffee shop for about forty-five minutes. He finally came through the doors and took the seat opposite me. We exchanged some small talk for a few minutes before he asked, "What's on your mind?"

I got right to the point. "I want to lead the youth here at the church."

He arched a brow. "I never took you for one who wanted to get into that part of ministry."

"I think I can help these kids," I said, smiling. "They need someone to be honest with them about what life is really like. I can do that."

After talking for nearly an hour, he agreed to put me on staff as the youth pastor.

"It doesn't pay much," he said, laughing. "Are you sure you want to do this?"

I chuckled. "Pastor Juan, I'm not doing this for the money. These kids need help. They need the truth."

So, the next day I took over as the youth pastor. My old buddies would be shocked. Me, a youth pastor. Back in the day I was so hardcore in that lifestyle of selling drugs, drinking, and sleeping around that no one in their right mind, including me, would have predicted that I'd be a youth pastor. In prison, I was part of the Aryan Brotherhood and the only influence we had on kids was, "If it ain't white, it ain't right." Thank the Lord I didn't see color anymore, just Jesus's blood that covers all.

Months later, I sat home one night watching some mindless show on television when someone knocked on the door. I wasn't expecting anyone, so I thought it might be one of the kids from youth group who needed to talk. I put the television on mute and hollered, "Hang on." I opened the door to see two men wearing sunglasses and dark suits. To say I was shocked is an understatement. "Hey boys, what can I do for ya?"

The taller of the two introduced himself as Ramey and the other as Hector. "We'd like a moment of your time."

"Sure, come on in." I said, motioning them toward the living room.

They sat on opposite ends of the couch. Ramey laid a large three-ring binder between them.

"Can I get ya something to drink?"

33

After they declined, I plopped into my recliner and said, "What can I do for ya?"

Ramey stood, clicked off the television with the remote on the end table next to me, and sat again. "We want you to go back in."

"Into what?"

"The motorcycle gang."

I stood and paced. "I don't think so." I stopped pacing and looked at both of them. "I've changed. I work for the church. I want nothing to do with that." I resumed pacing. "I did my time. I don't want to live like that anymore. I've given my life back to Jesus." I stopped. Pleaded with my eyes. "I can't. I just can't."

Ramey stood. "You don't have a choice. Now sit. We need to talk." As he spoke, he grabbed the three-ring binder. "Sit." After I did, he opened the folder that he had placed on the coffee table. "We've been tracking you while you've been on probation. We think you moved into town to start another gang. The Banditos moved into town last month. Now you move into town. We think you're here to start a rival gang." I opened my mouth to speak, but he held up a hand to stop me. "So, we want you to go back in."

"But I'm not interested."

He ignored my comment and continued talking. "We want you to move to Wittmann, just thirty miles northwest of here. No one will suspect what's going on."

34

I really didn't want to do this. When I got out of jail, I had two choices: go back in right away to Smitty and live in a clubhouse for $100 a month or find Jesus. I told Smitty I wanted to find Jesus. He was okay with that and my days as a motorcycle club member were over. At least that's what I thought.

The Feds had put me in a halfway house, got me a job as a line cook for a twenty-four hour eatery. Then I landed the job at the church. Life was good and these guys were about to muck it up. I learned while in prison that you couldn't say no to the Feds. They basically own you and Ramey didn't believe that I was keeping my nose clean.

He flipped through the binder, showing me that they had been tracking me. They had aerial photos of this place, as well as the last place I lived before it burned down. He also showed me schematics with the entries marked, and other things I couldn't believe they knew about Sissy and me.

I leaned back in my recliner and sighed. "Okay, boys. Here's how we need to do it." I leaned forward. "I'll start my own club, but I want to call Smitty and let him know. He and I talked right after I got out and I told him I didn't want back in. He told me to come back to him when I changed my mind."

They exchanged a glance and Ramey spoke. "I don't think you need to talk with Smitty."

"I'm telling you that I do. Smitty and I go way back. I can't start a club without him knowing. That breaks the code bikers have."

35

Ramey shook his head. "You have to do it our way or you'll be in violation of your probation. We'll have you back in prison tomorrow."

"I'm telling ya boys, Smitty will know something's up if I don't talk to him. You'll blow this right from the start."

Hector, who had been quiet since they arrived nearly an hour ago, spoke up. "If Smitty doesn't agree, you still need to start your own club."

"Smitty will agree. You can count on it."

The next day I called Smitty. He was happy to hear from me.

"You done being a Jesus freak?" he said, laughing.

"I guess I am. I thought that was the lifestyle for me, but it's not. I've come to believe bikers are better people than Christians." Truth was, at times I missed Smitty. He was one of the gentlest, nicest people I've ever met.

Smitty said, "I knew you'd be back. Someone like you can never leave this life behind. You'll be a biker forever."

"I know, I know. That's why I wanted to call you. I need my brothers."

"Well, come down to the clubhouse tonight and we'll figure this out." He chuckled. "You still got your cut, right?"

"Of course," I said, laughing. "Just because I loved Jesus, I didn't throw away my cut."

Smitty, there's one more thing. I want to open my own club. I'm too used to being a boss and I know myself well enough that I won't do well playing second fiddle to someone else."

"You can't do that," Smitty said. "We've got too many of those damn renegades starting their own club. Be a support club for a while and then we'll patch the whole club at the same time. How's that sound?"

"Works for me."

We talked another twenty minutes ironing out some of the details for me to start a support group for The Chosen Ones. Smitty offered me five support club options and I decided on the Jilted Jokers. During the next two weeks while I waited for the Feds to come back, I rounded up my old boys.

It was back on.

I was torn inside. I really had given my life back to the Lord. I also was still paying for my past sins. Sissy and I spent a lot of hours during those two weeks talking about how we could pull this off. About how we could live a double life. About how we could be true to ourselves and our faith while giving the Feds what they needed.

When Ramey and Hector returned we outlined what Smitty had said. They agreed to do it this way. So we moved to Wittmann, and fell in love with the place immediately. I know this sounds cliché, but we fell in love with the place the moment we rode into town. This quaint little town of about 1,000 people was just right for us to do what we needed to do and stay below the radar.

Wittmann is located along U.S. Route 60. The town is situated in what is considered an area of rapid growth. A new elementary school was built in the mid-2000s to accommodate an influx of students. The highway also was widened.

This seemed like the perfect place.

For a time it was.

With money from the Feds, we bought a bar. Big surprise. With my experience, I could run a bar in my sleep. And many nights I felt like I did. The place we bought, on the outskirts of town along the highway, was in shambles. The place was so bad that we stripped everything to the studs and rebuilt it. We named the bar *Toque del Cielo*, which means "Heaven's touch" in Spanish. We put up glass along one wall to make the place look better. We brought in a new bar that ran the length of the back wall. The front and opposite side wall were covered with wood planks that we salvaged from a home that was torn down a few blocks away. We built booths along the wood-planked wall and high tops along the glass. Tables filled the rest of the place. We had thirty different beers on tap and every kind of bottled alcohol you could imagine. When we finished, our bar was the talk of the town. About 100 people lined up the first night.

As we moved closer to the opening date, things were moving along fine. But of course, dealing with inspections, etc., is enough to drive a man to drink. I was still torn about all of this. We—Sissy and me —signed up for a three-year commitment. Three years. At first, that seemed like a long time. In reality three years is just a little over 1,000 days. When I looked at it like that, I knew I—we—could do it. In the past I had done this stuff by myself. Now, I had a girlfriend I wanted to marry, so I wasn't alone. And I had Jesus. While Smitty may have thought I gave up Jesus to be part of the club again, what he didn't know is that Jesus was a bigger part of my life than he had ever been.

We finished the bar in what seemed like record time. We worked eighteen hours a day for two months.

Opening night, I stood behind the bar and thought, "This is it. I'm back in my old lifestyle. Please, Jesus, don't leave me here. Protect me and Sissy while I do this work." I wish I could've prayed with the guys, but that would have blown my cover.

The first customer walked in a few minutes later and I started a journey that would take a drastic turn I never saw coming.

Chapter 3

A Thief Among Us

I loved my guys, plain and simple. I would have died for them, and I almost did a few times. I knew in my heart they would have died for me. Bikers are brothers, sometimes more so than any sibling any of us may have had. Guys join a biker club for a couple of reasons: camaraderie, brotherhood, love, and support. Others, like first responders and war vets, join up for the adrenaline rush.

Despite being a war vet and undercover for the Feds, I enjoyed the guys because they knew how to treat each other. Bylaws do exist and along with it, a code of honor. For instance, you can't lie. You just can't. If a biker is caught lying about something, he gets the tar beat of him, no questions asked. Now, someone in the club has to catch the guy in a lie before that happens. But that doesn't happen often. We lived by the old adage: a man's word is his bond.

Yes, we did crazy stuff like pull guns and knives on people. Intimidation is a big part of the tactics used by biker clubs, be it The Forsaken Ones, Banditos, Hell's Angels, Warlocks, or Outlaws, to name a few. One thing each group has in common is the brotherhood among its members.

So when prodded by the Feds to start another group, it wasn't much of a stretch for me to step into that role. I'm comfortable in that setting. And so are the guys who belong to clubs. We know how to treat people, how to talk with people, how to care for each other, to look out for each other.

Instead of turning your head or slipping away when you see a biker the next time, watch how they interact, not just with each other, but others they cross paths with. Unless, of course, the bikers have rolled into a place to "take care of business." If that happens, high tail it out of the there to protect yourself and your loved ones.

If you saw me and my guys, you might have thought that in some regards we were "normal" people. Most of us had jobs. Sissy and I owned the bar. A number of the guys worked there. A few others worked at places around town, like the automotive place or a convenience store. Yes, we drank—a lot—and some of the guys chased women. Drugs at the club were not permitted. We had a no pill and no powder policy. Away from the club, some of the guys did coke, meth, and heroine, but they were not allowed to do it while at the club. Drinking, chasing women, and doing drugs happen among society's upstanding people too. I don't think you'd have to look too far to find a group of lawyers, athletes, or even cops or fireman who did the same things as us.

41

I know I use "we" a lot. But it's appropriate. We (there I go again) do things as a team, or in the very least, pairs. If you saw one of the members of our club at the store, another was probably nearby.

Five of us patched together as the Jilted Jokers: Trent, Dick, Dough Boy, Willy, and me—"the fantastic five," someone once said. We certainly were quite the crew. Our guys swore to protect each other until the day we die.

I enjoyed being around Trent. He was a good kid and worked at a convenience store. He was good until he got a girlfriend. Women just ruined him. For whatever reason, when he had a girlfriend he'd be drunk and high all the time. Without one, he pretty much kept his nose clean— literally. When we patched Trent, we burned him in because he couldn't get beat due to an eye injury. He was about medium height, bald, and sleeved. He also smoked like a chimney.

Willy, my vice president, was a master mechanic. He could fix just about any kind of motor you took him. I remember seeing him working a motor from a 1920s Huckster, one of those trucks that people sold fruits and vegetables from. He was tough but fair to his customers. He told me once that people often took advantage of him when he first started working on engines. After years of being ripped off, he put his foot down. He'd take payment after he finished if he knew you. If he didn't, the person had to pay half up front. When they balked, he'd say, "That's the way it is." Because of his reputation, most paid the "down payment." Short and stocky, Willy got along with everyone despite only taking a bath or shower once a week. I don't know how others tolerated the smell, particularly the women.

Dick moved into our area just so he could patch with us. When he first started hanging out with us, he lived closer to the Phoenix house and should have probated with them. But he wanted to patch with us, so he rented a small house on the outskirts of town. His dad passed while he probated and we gave him a full military funeral. Dick was a good guy, but he didn't have the spine to be a bad guy. But if I told him to swing, he'd do it. Bottom line, he was a good soldier, but not a good leader. Short and frail, he looked like Mick Mars of Motley Crue from about 1987 when he had the long black handlebar mustache and goatee.

Dough Boy was the tallest one in the group. He hated it when I asked what the weather was like up there. Most people liked him because he was quiet and polite. He always said "please," "thank you," and answered with a "yes, sir" or "yes, ma'am." The women adored him. This one I got. For a biker, he took good care of his body. He also had one of the weirdest laughs you ever heard. It was more like a cackle than a laugh.

Very little about this ordeal was normal. To a non-believer it would appear a series of extraordinary circumstances. Some might have chalked it up to destiny. To Sissy, and me though, we could see God's hand in things that didn't seem right to others. For instance, I'd been a probate for the Jilted Jokers for about six months when I got a call for me and the boys to head to Phoenix. That happened enough times that we didn't think anything of it. We all jumped on our bikes and rolled into the Phoenix clubhouse about an hour and a half later.

The moment I stepped off my bike, Music Man, a guy I'd known for a long time, thrust a patch into my hand and asked, "Do you want this?"

I knew what this meant. You held onto the patch while four or five guys beat on you. I didn't expect this tonight or the moment I stepped off my bike. That didn't matter, though. I either had to grab the patch or get back on my bike and ride away. When you grab the patch, you can't let go. If you do, you're not man enough to patch. I grabbed the patch and said, "Hell yeah, I do."

Then for the next ten minutes, patched bothers from the Phoenix house beat the crap out of me while I held onto that patch with a death grip. They kicked me in the groin, punched me in the gut, pounded on my ribs and arms, and smacked me in the face a number of times. I took it like a man. You have to. You can't whine. You can't try to get away from them. You take it. When they were done, I still held the patch, and one of them said, "He's in."

After me, they patched the rest of my guys. When they were done with those guys, we stayed for a little bit and drank with the guys from the Phoenix house. A few hours later, tired, beaten, and bruised, we rode home to our clubhouse and continued the celebration by drinking into the wee hours of the morning. I think I slept most of the next day, which isn't normal for any of us. One thing about bikers, we can drink but most are up early the next day. That might be the military training in us. You don't see many slackers in a biker club. Don't get me wrong; they do exist. But they are the exception and not the rule.

So, we patched in six months when it's supposed to take a year. Some of the patches in the Phoenix house got pissed off. They didn't like it, but Smitty was the boss and he put an end to their displeasure by saying, "Boys, I don't want to hear another word about it." When Smitty laid down the law like that, you never heard about it again. His word was the gospel.

One thing about being in a biker club is the community attitude. If a guy needed a $100 to pay his electric bill, we'd pass the hat and collect enough money for the guy. It's just what we did. Unfortunately, that same guy might come back the next month needing money again for the electric bill or maybe something else. And we'd pass the hat again. It got frustrating when we'd collect money for someone to cover a bill and two weeks later he'd be at the club getting drunk off his ass. Or he might land in jail and we'd collect money again to post his bail.

It baffled me how some guys never learned. The worst thing, though, was not being able to help these guys by telling them about Jesus. Some days that tore me up inside. Sissy and I had the answer all along and we couldn't say a word.

When a brother needed help, we took care of him. At times I wondered why society, particularly the church, wasn't more like this. People may think we're just a bunch of hoodlums without any brains.

Really, though, we're like any other business in the U.S. We have goals, deadlines, and different personalities. Some guys were quiet. Some couldn't keep their mouth shut. Some couldn't hold their liquor. Some even cheated on their girlfriend or wife. And some got cheated on. We had accidents. People died. Sometimes our own. Life in the club was pretty much a reflection of society.

One time, a tornado hit the home of a chapter boss in West Texas. Hundreds of bikers rolled into town to help him. I remember pulling in front of what used to be a house. He stood among the rubble. I walked up to him, a guy I had never met, and put my arm around his shoulder. I gave him a squeeze. He turned and looked at me, his eyes wet with tears. "I knew you'd come."

"No better place right now than to be here to help you and your family," I said, choking back tears myself.

We dug in right away, sifting through the ruins practically non-stop. Not much was left of the house, and I think we recovered less than a crate of personal belongings. While the boys carefully worked their way through wood, glass, and chunks of concrete, the girls went to various stores in a nearby town and bought hundreds of dollars worth of gift cards.

Not only did the tornado destroy this guy's house, but it also blew away his bike. A brother needs a ride so someone from another chapter went home, got his extra bike, and gave it to the chapter boss who lost his.

Bikers can be tough for sure, but in situations like this, it wasn't uncommon to see a brother shed a tear or two. Or a lot in the case of the guy who lost his house. His "Ol'lady" got pretty emotional too when she received the gift cards. She had a difficult time saying thank you through her sobs.

We also put together a run and raised close to $85,000. All of this in three days.

That's what it can be like to be part of a motorcycle club. Of course, that's a hint of the good stuff that we do for each other when someone is in trouble. But, it's not always all good. We have problems too.

We soon discovered that we had a crook in the club. Some might think we were all crooks based on the activities we were involved in, but as I said, we lived by a code of honor. Our crook was a guy by the name of Freddie, a friend of my vice president Willy. Freddie stole a lot of money from the club. To the tune of $45,000. We were livid when we discovered what he did. We tried to find him. When we couldn't, we went to the cops. That sounds funny, I know. But we wanted some help finding him. The cops came back with a list of twenty-five known addresses Freddie had used in the last nine months. We never did find him, and the last we heard the Feds found Freddie barricaded with his family in a house in Florida.

We had no way of knowing that Freddie was a thief when he first visited the club. He came with Willy that night so he could check us out and possibly probate. That's how it works; a patched brother will bring in a friend. While the guy is checking us out, we're checking him out too. If someone wants to probate, we keep him around as much as we can. Get them to talk. After they leave for the night, we'd sit around and compare notes to see if we could catch the guy in a lie—about anything. Remember, lying is not tolerated. After ninety days, if a guy wanted to probate, we owned him for a year. If I called a probate at 2:00 a.m. and said get to the clubhouse right away, he had to come. It didn't matter if his wife or kids were sick or even in the hospital; he was required to come to the clubhouse. Or do whatever I ordered him at any time of the day.

A probate also had to keep his mouth shut. They were never allowed to discuss club business with anyone. A probate was required to learn the names, occupations and hobbies of all the members, and attend all events. In fact, probates worked the bar, the gate or security at events so the patched brothers could drink and socialize.

All of this was done to teach a probate how to respect others in the club, as well as the property girls. Respect was huge. Almost as huge as not lying.

Introductions were simple too. The probate was to introduce themselves as such for the name of the motorcycle club. Beyond that, they weren't supposed to talk much. As for nicknames, those were given based on the person's physical attributes and/or attitude.

48

The probation time was typically a year, but could be extended if a guy screwed up. As a probate, the person had no rank or privileges. Truth is, a probate started at the bottom of the chain. And they had to earn their way up and in.

Freddie seemed a nice enough guy right away. He looked like a biker for sure. Big, with a belly to match, long black hair tied in a ponytail, but with a full set of teeth. Willy vouched for him, so he became a probate. Everything seemed fine for a few weeks. Soon after we started the club, we rolled into town one night to hang out at one of the town's two bars. We quietly walked in and sat in the back booth in the corner near the kitchen door. We'd been there a while when some guy started running his mouth about one of our girls, Missy, Trent's woman. He went off about how much she was a slut and that he shared her with his friends. Trent naturally got pissed. We did our best to keep Trent off the guy and we eventually went back to the clubhouse. We kept drinking, of course.

Suddenly, Freddie jumped up and said, "We need to go back and kick that guy's ass." He started out the door.

I looked at Willy, shrugged, and stood and headed for my bike, saying, "Okay boys, let's roll."

When we returned to the bar, Freddie burst through the door yelling for the wiseass, calling him every name you could imagine, and some names I'd never heard before. The bartender, a woman in her mid-thirties, screamed, "He's not here!"

That didn't stop Freddie and he bolted through the kitchen door, still screaming. I stopped at the bar and said to the woman, "Keep serving or you're next. Got it?"

She nodded and I headed into the kitchen, hoping the guy wasn't in there. Thank goodness he wasn't. Freddie was so riled up at this point that he probably would have killed the guy. And that would have been hard to explain.

Straddling the fence was a tricky situation for me in times like this. I had to *act* bad, but I couldn't be *too* bad. I could only do so much, but I had to do enough so the guys would respect me as the boss. Just not enough to get in trouble. It sounds crazy, but I had to keep my nose clean with the law to make this work. If I got busted, it was over. Not just for me, but for Sissy too.

With all this going through my mind, I looked up and Freddie had the cook pinned against the wall about two feet off the floor. Dough Boy, who followed Freddie into the kitchen, had a gun jammed into the guy's side. He didn't say a word until he looked at me, then in broken English he said, "I don't know. I don't know where he is."

Dough Boy jammed the gun deeper into the guy's ribs.

"Please don't kill me." He scissor-kicked his feet, which didn't do any good. I hoped he knew better than to kick Freddie. That would have been bad too.

"Shut up," I screamed. "We know you know where he is and you better tell us."

50

The guy opened his mouth to interrupt me and Freddie punched him. "Don't open your mouth when he's talking. Understand?" Wide-eyed, the cook nodded. Two of his teeth fell to the floor. I kicked one of them under the sandwich table.

"Now, let's try this again." I took a step closer, praying the whole time that Dough Boy didn't pull the trigger or that Freddie didn't choke the guy to death. "When my buddy here puts you back on the floor, I'm gonna give you a card and I want you to understand one thing. When you see that little rat hole again, you call me. Okay?"

"Si, si," he said, his voice trembling.

"Put him down," I said.

Freddie let go and the guy collapsed on the floor.

"You guys get out of here. I want to have a private conversation about making sandwiches."

After Freddie and Dough Boy left, I pulled the cook to his feet. He was still shaking pretty hard. Part of me felt bad for him. This guy didn't deserve what Freddie just did. "Listen, just do as I say and everything we be okay. Got it?" He nodded and I walked out.

Freddie and Dough Boy stood at the end of the bar eyeing the other customers who were surprisingly quiet.

"Okay boys, let's go." I turned to the bartender and said, "Give us three Yuenglings and we'll be on our way."

"I don't think so," Freddie said. "I want to drink here."

I took a spot at the bar and said, "Okay, let's drink."

The bartender, bless her heart, came over and asked in a calm tone of voice, "What'll it be?"

Freddie ordered enough alcohol to supply a small infantry and added, "And we're not paying for it."

The bartender didn't flinch. She simply gave us what we wanted.

I wanted to shake my head. I couldn't believe how this had gone down. But that's what bikers do sometimes and I had to play along. The bartender brought me a beer, and knowing the cops would be here soon, I celebrated our victory over the cook by taking a long draw on my cold one.

Sure enough, about ten minutes later, this cop comes in and sits down next to me at the bar. Without saying a word, he ordered a drink. After the bartender brought his draft and moved away, he turned to me. "What's going on here?"

"Nothing. Just sitting here having a drink."

"Seems awful quiet in here," he said, taking a peek over his shoulder at the people sitting behind us. "You know anything about that?"

I smiled. "Maybe they're enjoying their drinks."

He chuckled. "You think so?"

"That's my guess." I turned to face him for the first time. Big guy. Bigger than I thought. And for the first time I was glad Freddie was with me. "Why don't you ask them?"

"I don't think I need to." He took a sip of his beer. "I know what's going on here. I'm just glad that no one got hurt."

I held up my beer to clink his glass and said, "Me too."

For the next thirty minutes we touched on a variety of subjects. The weather. The Diamondbacks baseball team. The upcoming football season and the expectations of the college and pro teams. After I ordered my third beer, he encouraged me to go outside to continue our talk. I turned to Freddie and Dough Boy and ordered them to follow us out.

When we stepped outside into an unusual chilly evening for late summer, the blinds on the windows snapped shut and I heard the deadbolt snapping into place. "Nice move," I said to the cop.

"Just trying to protect the honorable citizens of Wittmann," he said, smiling.

I nodded and ordered my boys back to the clubhouse.

That made us think that Freddie really wanted to be one of us. He earned his way in and we trusted him with more and more responsibilities, like picking up kegs for the bar, running checks around town to businesses that were working on the bar. Then he asked us for $20,000 to cover a doctor bill for one of his kids. He made up some story that he got stuck with the bill because insurance at his new job hadn't kicked in yet. That was a lot of money to give a probate, but our code is to help each other. I got the money from the vault at the clubhouse and handed the money to Freddie. I don't even think he said "thank you."

A few weeks later we were all at the club for a fundraiser. Being new in the town, we wanted to make a good impression on the locals. We decided to have a fundraiser and donate all the proceeds to the local scouts clubs. We put up a bouncy house for the little kids, a dunk tank, ring toss and other carnival games for both kids and adults. I can't remember how much we raised that day.

Midway through the day, I noticed Freddie wasn't there so I called him a few times. Each time he had some kind of excuse. Finally I said, "If you want to be part of this club you need to get down here."

"I do, I do," he said. "But my wife hurt her ankle earlier today and I'm trying to keep her comfortable."

"I don't care, man. You need to get down here."

A little while later he showed up. He acted weird the whole time he stayed, which may have been an hour. I caught him inside the clubhouse and asked him to follow me outside for a chat. When he resisted, I blurted, "What, you got your ol' lady in the car?" When I saw his reaction, I shook my head. We spoke for a few minutes outside and then I told him to get his wife back home and take good care of her.

The next day I called two or three times to check on Freddie and see if his wife's ankle was better. I didn't hear back from him so I called a few times the next day. Again, no answer. On the third day, Dough Boy, Trent, and me rode out to his house. The place was empty. Not even a curtain was left. Apparently while we hosted the fundraiser, Freddie was packing up his house to skip town.

Willy was steaming mad. He brought Freddie in and vouched for him. Then Freddie made him look bad. You just don't do that to a brother. It took Willy a couple of months to get over what Freddie did.

Freddie ripping us off put the screws to us. Despite having a successful bar, we were in the hole some $100,000 dollars for the renovations we made before we opened. And we still had more fixing-up to do. We struggled for months and never really did catch up.

All because we let someone in who was better than me at playing both sides of the fence.

Chapter 4

It's All Good

"Let's roll," I yelled to the boys and headed toward the door.
Trent, Willy, and two new guys—Spade and Old Man—followed me out
the door.

Smitty had just called like he was accustomed to doing and asked
me and my boys to help him do some work around the Phoenix house.
For some reason when Smitty needed help around his clubhouse, only
one guy would show. Unfortunately, it was never the same guy so
Smitty didn't have at least one person to count on.

I can honestly say that I never let Smitty down. When he called,
we rolled out. If he called and wanted donuts from the place two blocks
from his club, I'd drive the ninety minutes to get the donuts and take
them to him. He never asked that of me, but I would have done it.

Our Jilted Jokers club quickly became a group of guys who
Smitty could count on. He needed that. A biker for more than thirty
years, he'd pretty much seen it all, including the guys from his own club
pretty much disappear. I liked Smitty a lot and I felt bad for him at the

same time. I couldn't understand how his own people could abandon such a sweet guy. It didn't make sense to me and it wasn't right.

When we rolled up to his place, it was mid-afternoon in late summer and certainly not the best time to work outside. But Smitty was digging up God-knows-what with a shovel near the corner of his club. He looked like he was about to keel over. I jumped off the bike, hustled over, and took the spade from his hand. "What're ya doing? Trying to kill yourself?"

He looked up at me with exhaustion in his eyes. "Give me the shovel," he said, trying to take it from me.

I put the shovel behind my back out of his reach. "Move out of the way and let me do the digging."

"You think I'm too old for this?"

I put my hand on his shoulder. His shirt was soaked. "You know I can't lie to you."

He smiled.

"Now tell me what we're digging here."

He pointed to the hole. "What does it look like to you?"

I looked into the hole and arched a brow. Within the pit lay one big snake. "You can't be serious."

"Yup," Smitty said. "Found it out on the porch when I came out to get something from the bike. It was on the top step, rattling. So I went back inside, got my shotgun, and killed it. One of the biggest dang rattlers I've seen in my entire life. I bet that thing was a good seven feet."

I couldn't tell how long it was, but the fattest part was about nine inches around. "Why are you burying it? Why don't you just throw it in the trash?"

"And let the dang raccoon pull it out later tonight? Nah. I figured I'd just bury him."

I shook my head. "Let me finish this here for you. Go inside and get cooled off. It'll just take me a few minutes."

He reached for the shovel again. "No. I'll finish."

"If you won't let me finish this, why'd you call us up here?"

He laughed. "Why don't you guys fix the roof and I'll finish with this hole."

"You're kidding me?" I shielded my eyes and looked at the roof. "In this heat?"

"I can dig this hole but I can't get on the roof. Too old. I might fall off." He laughed again. "You boys work on the roof and when I'm done here I'll go inside and get the beers ready."

"You're something else," I said to him, and then to the guys who stood nearby watching the exchange, "Okay boys, you heard the man. We're on the roof. Dough Boy, grab the ladder from the shed. Willy, get up there and tell me what we need to fix the leak."

"Yes, Boss," said Trent as he motioned for Willy and Spade to follow him.

To Old Man, I said, "Go keep Smitty company."

I ambled over to my bike and pulled out my work gloves and a hanky. I wiped the sweat that covered my face. *This is going to be a brutal afternoon*, I thought.

I cussed Smitty numerous times while on the roof. I was still at a loss as to why he wanted us to fix the roof today. The temperature was close to 100 degrees. An hour later, we took a much-needed break. I pulled out my cell to call Sissy while the others went inside for one of those beers Smitty was supposed to have ready for us.

Sissy didn't sound happy when she answered.

"What's wrong, Babe?"

"You don't want to know."

"Well then, don't tell me. I just wanted—"

"You won't believe what happened," was how she started. And for the next ten minutes she went off about how she caught one of the girls in the bathroom with one of the customers and then the pain-in-the-butt fire marshal stopped by. The girl getting caught didn't surprise me. This particular young lady was known for being friendly with the customers, but we hadn't been able to catch her. Until now. The fire marshal stopping by again ticked me off. I couldn't tell if he dropped by as often as he did because he had a crush on Sissy or that he was trying to nail us on some bull crap violation. Today, I got my answer. It seemed he wanted to get us shut down.

"What are we going to do?" she said. "They'll shut us down if we don't get these things fixed."

"Babe, don't worry about it," I said, wondering exactly where we'd get the money. The list was pretty long and this just might be the end of it soon after we opened. "We'll get it fixed."

"Freddie really screwed us big time."

I couldn't argue with her on that one. Running off with $45,000 really did put us in a bind. I figured the visit from the fire marshal was just a little bump in the road.

"You didn't hear me," she said. "We have eighty-seven violations and he gave us a week to get them fixed. We don't have the money or the time to—"

"Sissy," I said, raising my voice. "What does Philippians 4:13 say?"

"I can do all things through Christ who strengthens me."

"You know it, so now believe it."

"But—"

"No buts. God wants us to trust him in all situations, not just the ones we are comfortable with." I heard her sigh on the other end. "Has he let us down yet?" She sighed again and I chuckled. "Say something."

"Alright."

"That's it. Alright?" I wiped my face.

Trent came out and held up a beer for me. "Need one, Boss?"

I held up a forefinger. "I gotta go. We'll be back by dark and get to work. In the meantime, pray." I clicked off the call, wondering if I could believe what I had just told Sissy. Could I really believe that anything is possible no matter how impossible? People share testimonies about the impossible coming true. I've heard quite a few myself over the years. But did I have the faith to walk through something like that and be able to share it later? As much as the bar was killing us, we needed it to stay open. It was a gold mine for the Feds to keep track of the players and the events as we helped them build their cases. One nice benefit of being undercover was all the cool gadgets I got to use. I probably had more than Dick Tracy ever did.

On the ride back to our house in Wittmann, I got a text on my private phone from Ramey, one of my handlers. I didn't see the text until we parked the bikes at the clubhouse. He wanted to meet right away. I texted back that I couldn't because I needed to get to the bar to look over some paperwork. He replied right away: Meet at 9:00 p.m. and gave a location. *Great*, I thought. There's no making these guys happy.

I went by the bar, got a bite to eat, and talked with Sissy. She seemed less frantic. So I met Hector and Ramey at the predetermined location. We met in some of the strangest locations, and this was no exception. I had trouble finding this little park that was in the middle of some neighborhood on the northwest part of town. The park wasn't bad, but to have a biker roll through wasn't a subtle way of getting together at this location. I spotted Hector and Ramey right away at one of those

61

green metal picnic tables that are bolted to a slab of concrete. And someone I didn't know sat with his back toward the parking lot. He wore a three-piece patch.

After shaking hands with my handlers, they introduced the other guy as Red.

"Nice to meet you," I said while I took a seat on the bench opposite him. He didn't say anything, which I thought was odd, so I turned to Ramey, "What's so urgent?"

Just then, Hector's phone rang. He excused himself from the table and walked a few feet away and out of earshot. A moment later he motioned for Ramey to join him. That left me and mute at the table. I tried to engage in conversation, but he didn't want anything to do with me. He kept looking at Hector and Ramey, who were circling an imaginary hole in the ground while Hector kept his phone pressed to his ear.

Finally, Red looked at me and said, "Why are you doing this?"

"Doing what?"

"You know."

"No, I don't know." I interlocked my fingers and rested my hands on the table. "So why don't you tell me."

He stood and stepped away from the bench. I sized him up. About my height, but a little heavier. Lots of tats. No rings on his fingers. That was good, particularly if we were about to knuckle up. No signs of a gun or knife, which didn't mean anything. Guys know how to hide those pretty good.

I stood and stepped in front of him. When he didn't react, I thought that nothing would happen. I was wrong.

"I don't think you can do this," Red said, half-smiling.

Frustrated, I snapped back. "Do what?"

"Quit playing games with me."

"Look buddy, I don't know who you are or what you want, but I'm not the one playing games here."

He balled a fist and took a step closer. When I didn't move, or even flinch, he balled the other fist. "I'm gonna give you a beating like you've never had."

"Bring it on." And I meant it. I learned a long time ago that you never backed down. That was a sign of weakness. I've had guys who outweighed me by 100 pounds or more back down when I didn't flinch. It wasn't of weakness on their part, but would have been on mine. So, I stood my ground with this guy Red.

He stared at me probably longer than it seemed and he finally said, "That's it then." He unballed his fists. "We're good."

Hector and Ramey walked back and sat at the table. Red said, "He's your guy. He won't crack," and joined them.

Trying to figure out what had just happened, I stayed on my feet in case Red wanted to change his mind and make a quick move. I looked at Hector and asked, "What the hell is going on?"

Ramey spoke, "We've put guys in before and they committed suicide. You've been in six months at this point and we wanted to see if you could handle this."

"Wouldn't it have been nice to do this *before* you put me in?"

"That obviously doesn't work or guys wouldn't have killed themselves."

"Finding that out now doesn't do any good. I'm stuck." I finally sat next to Hector and across from Red. "You know I have to put in five years before I can retire. This was stupid." I started to walk away. "You boys just don't get it."

"Stop," Red said. "We're not done."

I spun back toward them. "Here we go again." I looked at Ramey, who had strangely been quiet tonight. "What do you have planned?"

"Nothing," he said. "Now sit. We have something serious to discuss." After I rejoined them at the table, he added, "By the way, Red is an undercover from New Mexico."

That certainly caught me off guard. "Out of state? What's he here for?"

"Well," Hector said, "we're opening up the case to cross state lines."

Red took over at that point and explained how he needed to get involved in the case as well. What the three had discovered as we built the case was that a lot was happening across state lines. Word got around about our dealings and the Mexican cartel wanted to get involved. I knew joining forces with the cartel would take the case to another level. Most people don't realize the Mexican mob is in just about every town in the U.S. That may sound scary to some, but the cartel has systemically infiltrated our society. The mob joined up with the biker clubs to sell dope, traffic stolen goods and sex slaves, deal high-powered assault weapons, and extort. Really, just about anything one can think of.

I really didn't like where this was going. Making the case bigger meant more guns, more drugs, and certainly more danger for Sissy and me. But we didn't really have any say in the matter. We couldn't say no. I know I had just passed their little test, but a very small part of me wondered what would have happened if I had failed. I felt like I had done a lot for these guys already. When they came to me to go in, Ramey and Hector knew practically nothing. They had one sheet of paper. Hell, they had more information on me when they came to the house the first time, a whole three-ring binder. About the guys they wanted me to rat, they had nothing.

By the time we finished, we provided more than 500 names with a list of offenses against each. I appreciated that they trusted me, but they ran me ragged. So now that I had spoon-fed a list of guys, along with their ranks in various clubs around the state, they wanted me to start rubbing elbows with the national bosses. I didn't think that would be a problem because of my relationship with Smitty. I also told them that we had a Valentine's Day regional event coming up in a couple of months and mentioned the national bosses were expected to be there.

"Good," Red said. "I'll be there too."

"So, why don't you rub elbows with them?"

"I'm not a chapter boss. You know how this works. Hierarchy is everything. Like in the military." I smiled at the comment while he continued. "It makes more sense for you to get close."

Hector chimed, "You see any problems?"

I shook my head. "Just keep the money coming so I can set up the deals you need me to make." I stood to leave.

"One more thing," Red said, flipping me a wad of cash, "here's ten grand to get the bar up to code. We know everything that goes on in the bar, even when you're not there." He smiled. "And we should talk about that. Things are going on that you should know about."

"Spill it."

"That's a conversation for another time. My number's in the middle of those bills. Call me sometime and we'll set up a time to meet." He stood. "Now, I gotta go. Time to meet the old lady for a late dinner."

He brushed past me and climbed into a convertible Alfa Romeo. Dang, I thought. Maybe I need to work for the Feds when this was all over. He backed out and sped off, spinning a little tire for show.

I waited a week to call Red, after we got all the stuff taken care of at the bar. Sissy was happy that night when I returned with the cash. When I showed her, she asked, "Did you knock off a bank?" I reassured her that I hadn't. The next day we called in various contractors, plumbers, and electricians that we needed. We promised each a bonus if they finished within a week. At times, we watched workers from three different companies scramble over top of each other to get their work done. Of course, one time I had to step in to stop a fight. It was obvious that they all wanted the bonus we promised. And they all made it. Thankfully, most of the workers spent their bonus by buying beer in the bar. So, we got back what we had paid out.

Before I called Red, I stood in the doorway of the office watching Sissy go over tapes. "God, you look beautiful."

Without looking up, "Not here."

"What? I just think you look beautiful. Why can't I tell you that?"

She stopped and gave me a tired look. "Like this?"

I held her gaze. "Even when you look exhausted."

"Go away so I can finish this."

I left and walked out back to call Red. He answered on the first ring. "I wondered when I might hear from your sorry butt."

"Thanks for the warm welcome."

"That's what I do. Greeting people warmly and making them feel loved."

"Well, golly gee thanks," I said with a hint of sarcasm.

"What's on your mind? I'm sure this isn't a social call."

67

"Could be. I have a handful of guys that I touch base with every day. I thought about adding you to the list, but after that greeting I'm not sure." I chuckled.

"I see that you can give it as good as you can take it."

For the next five weeks, we kept going about our business—running the bar and selling guns and dope while we counted down the days to the Valentine's Day event in Tucson, about a two-and-a-half hour ride from our club. Sissy and I had been together for a couple of years by now and celebrating the day of love was a big deal to her. I didn't get it the first year we were together. I got her a card, some roses, and took her to dinner. On the ride back to her place, she sat in the passenger seat of the car and asked, "That's it?"

"What?"

"Every cliché for Valentine's Day?"

Oh crap, here we go, I thought.

"You couldn't have thought of anything original. Not one single thing?"

I liked it when she got sassy, but now was not the time to bring that up. She was really ticked right now. "Well, Babe. I wanted to play it safe this year."

"Play it safe? Thanks a stinking lot."

We rode the last thirty minutes to her place in silence. When I pulled into the driveway, she jumped and slammed the door. I opened my door to get out and, walking past my door, she said, "Don't even bother." I closed the door, watched her walk inside, and then drove away.

So this year, I had something special planned when we got to the Valentine's Day bash. Every hour from noon until 8:00 p.m. one of the probates from our club was to walk up and give her a gift from me, even if I was standing next to her. The last gift was to be given to me so I could get down on one knee and propose. After the debacle two years prior, I'd learned my lesson and I wanted to make this day and every one after, special for her.

Valentine's Day proved to be a disaster. First, it was cold, which isn't common for that part of the state. The average high for the month of February is in the mid-sixties. We didn't set a record low that day, but I'm sure we got close to making the top ten coldest days in Tucson history. I think we hovered around twenty-eight degrees that day, cold enough to see your breath.

Second, the cold made the ride miserable. Riding in cold like that is hard on the body, particularly your fingers. If you have a shield, that helps keep the wind off your face and chest, but it still can be pretty brutal. That day, I alternated putting one hand inside my jacket while holding the handlebars with the other. Still, my fingers were pretty stiff when we rolled into the campsite.

By this time we had about fifteen guys in the club, most of them probates. But they still had to go with us. One guy, Taker, who got his nickname because he had the habit of taking food off other people's plate before they were finished eating, was pissed off because he had tickets to the Suns game in Phoenix. His wife gave them to him as a birthday present. That didn't matter, we reminded him. When we ride, we all ride. No excuses.

I told him, "If you're in, you're all in or not at all."

So he joined us while his wife went with a girlfriend to the game. Needless to say, when we arrived at the event, like the rest of us, he was cold and wet. And instead of drinking, he had to work. I'm sure he would have preferred to drink away his frustration, but duty called.

We rolled up to the campgrounds and the first thing we saw was a huge, pink, "VD" sign above the gate. That's a biker for you, I thought.

Sissy and I wandered around the grounds for a little while. This was not only a perfect opportunity to meet the big bosses, but also guys from the other clubs. The goal was to patch as The Forsaken Ones and not be a support club any more. But we needed the full support of the other brothers. If even one member votes against you, you don't get patched. We still had about half a year before we could patch, which probably would take place at a regional event at the beginning of summer. This gave us plenty of time to get to know other guys in other clubs. So, like a politician, I started glad-handing that day. I certainly spent more time shaking hands and introducing myself than drinking beer. Sissy spent part of the day drinking with Willy's girlfriend and playing some kind of bingo game that involved a chicken and a hole in a piece of plywood. Throughout the day, she received her valentine gifts, some of which were ruined by the time they got there. Each time, she texted to find out where I was, then showed up to give me a kiss.

Just after dark I ran into Smitty and we talked for a little while before I asked if I could meet the big boys.

"I like the way you think, Boss."

"Whaddaya mean?"

"You understand how all this works, that you need to make good with the big boys."

He jumped down off the edge of the picnic table and motioned for me to follow. We moved through the packed crowd. A band started to crank up a popular Led Zeppelin tune and I stopped to listen for a second. Smitty grabbed my arm and pulled me along. "You've got all night to listen to these guys. Now let's go."

I spent the next hour talking with the "big boys"—Tiger, Little Pointer, and Splash. At least we tried to talk with them. They weren't much for talking. Their deal was to stand around and intimidate people. That didn't work on me. I needed to position myself to get the Jilted Jokers patched. More important, I knew that I would eventually get pulled out after we got the Feds what they needed. But for the purpose of this meeting I had to make sure the Jilted Jokers were in.

You either hated or loved the new guard. No different than society, the new guys wanted to push out the old guys because they were all about money, money, money. Some guys liked that. The old guard particularly. They felt the old guys were being disrespected. And they were, for the love of money.

Tiger, a thin man with a long goatee and ponytail to match, was the national boss. He called the shots for the entire organization. A behemoth of a man named Little Pointer was Tiger's hang-around buddy. Whenever you saw Tiger, Little Pointer was nearby, usually no more than five or ten feet away. Tiger was relatively new in his position, less than two years, and was asserting himself as the new boss similar to a new CEO taking over at a long established company. The politics were the same.

Splash, a short guy with only a few teeth, the stereotypical biker, was the regional boss. He was the guy who would host the regional where we'd get patched. At least that was the plan, according to Smitty.

I turned on my secret recorder and listened to Smitty do most of the talking. I tried to chat up the guy about bikes and the event itself, but he didn't say much to me. When we walked away, Smitty said, "I think you're good."

"How can you say that?"

"He barely said a word to me."

"That's good news."

I smiled. Everything was going as planned, and no one was on to us.

The last guy showed up with Sissy's engagement ring. I said to Smitty, "Come on. I want you here for this." I took off walking faster than he could to keep up.

"Slow the hell down," he called out from behind. "What's the big hurry?"

I stopped and showed him the ring.

"Well, let's get moving then."

We found Sissy at one of the bars inside. I kissed her hard on the lips.

"Well, that's a greeting a woman could get used to."

With the smell of booze, urine and weed heavy in the air, I dropped to one knee and opened the box.

She shrieked and everyone within earshot turned in our direction.

"Will you marry me?"

She jumped off the barstool. "Yes, yes, yes, yes," she said in between kisses.

I slid the ring on her finger and whispered, "I will take care of you, always and forever."

"I know you will."

The euphoria from getting engaged that night didn't last long. We returned the next day from the Valentine's Day trip to discover our house had been hit, not the clubhouse, but the home that Sissy and I lived in. It's true that some bikers sleep at the club, but we didn't. For us, it was a place to hang out with friends and drink. The back door was standing wide open. I turned to Sissy and asked, "Did you leave the door open?" She replied that she hadn't and I told her to go back outside. I called Willy while I searched the house. It didn't look like anything was taken but someone had jimmied the door.

Sissy was shaken up and I was ticked off. I blew off some steam with a little rant. The next day Dick and I fixed the door. My first thought was Freddie had returned to clean us out. He knew where we kept our money so I moved it to a different hiding place.

Unfortunately that wasn't the only time we got hit. For the next six weeks, someone hit the house while we hosted dinner night at the club. Whoever jimmied a door or pried open a window never seemed to enter the house. To this day we're still not sure who was doing it. Or why. We had our suspicions about who it might be, but we could never confirm those thoughts.

To be honest, I got tired of coming home to find a door or window open. Finally I put a new probate—Double M because he looked like Mickey Mouse—in the house and ordered him to keep the lights off.

"If you hear anything, you call me," I instructed him.

I didn't hear from Double M and was glad to return home to all our windows and doors being in one piece.

For the next month, I put a probate in the house on dinner night and nothing ever happened again.

Thankful that we finally put an end to the break-ins, I focused my attention on the case, running the bar with Sissy, pulling more guys into the chapter, talking with Smitty about patching the chapter at the regional. Oh, I can't forget the most important thing—getting ready for the wedding.

Chapter 5

The Stress is Killing Me

In the months leading up to our wedding, we kept working on the club (there's always something that needs done, just like a house), organizing and planning the deals the Feds needed, working with the probates, and just being a badass whenever I needed to. Thankfully, that wasn't often.

One time, we heard a rival gang had rolled into town. One of our guys was out running an errand and saw a group of them stop at the bar where Freddie pinned the cook against the wall. Protocol was for their boys to call and let us know if they planned to stop in town. This courtesy call is supposed to be made to avoid bloodshed. Clubs and gangs don't like someone else rolling in on their turf. You just don't do that. If you roll in without making a call, you're looking for trouble. I was afraid that was the deal on this one. So I made a few calls, including one to Ramey, to see what the deal was. No one knew, so I made the decision to check it out.

Everyone jumped on their bike and headed out to the bar. Sure enough, about fifteen bikes belonging to their gang were parked outside. I motioned for us to roll past. We pulled into a convenience store about a mile down the road. I walked in to grab a pack of smokes while I thought about what to do next. I didn't want to knuckle up with these guys. We were making headway in the case, the wedding was coming up, and I would lose it all if something stupid happened. I went to pay for my cigarettes and a coke that I grabbed from the cooler. When I got to the register, the cashier had a shotgun leveled at me.

"Whoa, whoa," I said, backing away and raising my hands. "I just want to pay for my stuff."

He waved the shotgun in the direction of the door and told me to get out.

"Look, I just want to pay for my stuff. I don't want to cause any trouble. I just want to pay for my stuff."

"You guys came in here a little bit ago and tore up my store. Now get out of here."

"Wait a second," I said. "Do you remember what the patch on the back of the vests looked like?"

"No, I didn't get a look at it while they trashed my store. Took me an hour to put everything back."

I turned around. "Any chance this patch looks the same?"

"I told you, I didn't get a good look at it."

"Look, if we wanted to tear up your store," I said, turning back around, "why are the rest of my boys outside while I'm in here? Shouldn't we all be in here?" When he didn't answer, I continued, "Those guys who tore up your store are at the bar about a mile down the road. We rolled in here to run them out of town."

"Really?"

I could see his arms getting tired from holding the gun. "Let me pay for my stuff and me and my boys will go next door and wait for those guys to come out." He kept the shotgun aimed at my chest. "Okay?"

"Put the money on the counter and take your stuff and leave."

I put a $50 on the counter for stuff that cost less than $10, grabbed my stuff, and left.

"What was all that about, Boss?" Willy asked.

"Those guys down at the bar trashed his place a little while ago and he thought we came back to finish him off." I fired up my bike and motioned for the guys to follow me to a new waiting spot. When we rolled into the next place, a little farther down the road, a pair of bikers from the rival gang rolled past toward the bar. Willy started after them and I held him back. "Give 'em a minute. Let's see what happens."

When they got to the bar, one of the guys went inside and in a few minutes the entire group came out, jumped on their bikes, and headed our way. *Great*, I thought. This isn't how I wanted this to go down. It doesn't take a group of bikers to cover a mile on a flat, empty road. We lined up along the road and I yelled above the roar of the approaching bikes, "Remember boys, I swing, you swing; if I don't, you don't."

Much to my surprise, the rival gang rolled by without stopping. And without even a single middle finger from any of their members. I certainly expected the worst, but the best possible thing happened. "Thank you, Lord," I mumbled under my breath before ordering the boys back to the clubhouse.

Red started coming around about twice a month. I grew to like Red. He wasn't a true biker type, but he got it. Sadly, not everyone did. Some guys think they do and they will tell you that they do, but they don't. And they don't even know. Sad.

When Red came around, we'd sit for hours at the club drinking beer, playing pool, throwing darts, which I wasn't very good at, and talk about everything under the sun. He was a smart guy, probably college educated. I think he fit in because he knew how to talk to people. I don't ever recall him disrespecting anyone, male or female, to his or her face or even behind their backs. If we needed to talk about the case, we'd head down out of town to eat at a little diner along U.S. Route 60. When we first started going, I could tell our presence made the customers nervous. I caught them glancing our way a number of times and even saw a mother pull her child close into her. I smiled at her and nodded. She didn't acknowledge either.

Our waitress that first time was a little skittish too. Her hands shook when she took our drink orders, which she spilled when she put them on the table. By the time we left, she was obviously a lot less scared. She even cracked a joke with Red about his boots.

"We're not all bad, you know," he said.

"Well, you guys aren't, but we've had some pretty nasty guys come in here," she said.

The two chatted for a few minutes and at one point I thought Red might ask for her phone number. But she was right; there are some nasty guys out there in the motorcycle world. They proudly call themselves the one-percenters. Basically, a one-percenter is a hardcore biker belonging to a traditional style motorcycle club like ours, the Jilted Jokers. The term originated back in the 1950s when the American Motorcycle Association made the comment in which they stated that 99-percent motorcyclists were law-abiding citizens, implying that the last one percent were outlaws. Many in the one-percent club are not necessarily involved in organized crime or drug running. One may believe they are because of their "don't give a rat's ass" mentality.

I knew a number of the one-percenters, and the majority were good, decent people who happened to live a lifestyle that includes, bikes, brotherhood, loyalty, and a healthy dose of partying.

A one-percenter wears a special diamond patch on their cut. To be a one-percenter, the person must commit to a club and live for the club. A true one-percenter must protect anyone in the club at the cost of his own blood or life. It's the closest thing our modern society has to ancient "blood covenants." Like I've said before, it's a true brotherhood.

And I think that's why a great number of military vets gravitate to this lifestyle. It's the mindset they lived with when in the middle of war. The Marines live life by a "No man left behind" oath. The same is true with a one-percenter.

With the wedding now less than a month away, things were getting tight. Things at the bar weren't great. That added to Sissy's anxiety, so we decided to let someone else run the bar for a little while so we, mostly her, could focus on the final details for our nuptials. The Feds were also ramping up the investigation. I often heard from Ramey or Hector with new ideas and new orders. After one intense conversation with Ramey, Sissy lost it. A week before the wedding, she went off. I let her go and didn't say a word. I knew she'd been holding a lot in and needed to get it out. The stress on her was unreal. It's only by God's grace that she didn't crack under all the pressure. This was a woman who'd never seen hard drugs in her life, and now we're dealing dope like crazy. This was a woman who had seen weed before, but never seen guys smoke it nonstop. She told me once that she couldn't understand how the smokers could blaze up all day and then go out and ride. "In high school I was taught that marijuana slows your reflexes," she said one day. And this was a woman, who despite having an alcoholic mother and uncle, wasn't used to spending each day at a bar watching people

81

drink their life away and then at night watching people at the club do the same thing.

In my mind, she certainly was the closest thing on earth to an angel. And I got to marry her.

The day after her rant, I got a call from Ramey while fixing breakfast. He didn't even say hello. He started with, "You better get that girl of yours under control."

"What are you talking about?"

"I heard her rant last night."

"How?" I furrowed my brow.

"You left on your recorder." I started to say something but he kept going, this time his voice rising. "I know you guys are getting married in a week and you better get her under control or she is going to blow this case."

"She'll be fine," I said

"And what do you plan to do?" he said, still irritated. "I don't think you can keep her under control. You didn't even say a word."

"I didn't need to. She needed to vent and I listened. That's all that was about."

"I hope you're right. You don't want us to come in there and remove her, do you?"

That pricked my anger button. "If you know what's best for you, you'll leave it alone." I snapped my cell phone shut and tossed it on the counter.

"Who was that," Sissy asked as she sauntered into the room.

"Ramey."

"My favorite person." She kissed me on the cheek. "What did he want?"

"Nothing. Just going over some details for the next deal." I had to lie because she would've gone off on another rant. And I wondered for the first time if we really could do this for a full five years.

I woke the day of our wedding after just four hours of sleep. I slipped out of bed and pulled open the curtains. The sun was just coming up. I marveled at God's handiwork and gave him a silent prayer of thanks for Sissy, for keeping me safe, and for everything to come, good or bad.

Biker weddings usually take place at the club, and after much convincing so did ours. Sissy wanted to get married in a nearby country club. She wanted to tie the knot outside in a peaceful setting with summer flowers in bloom and a breeze lifting her veil. I liked the idea, but had to play the role—again—for this one. We compromised. Instead of just standing on the front steps of the club, the boys and me built a white arbor made of motorcycle parts on the bottom and flowers for the arch.

I showed up at the club at noon for our 4:00 p.m. wedding. When I rolled through the gate I couldn't believe how many bikes covered the grounds. The guys from our club were obviously invited, along with a few other select invitations, so we didn't plan for or expect a big wedding. Probably fifty to sixty at the most. There were at least that many bikes parked all over the gravel. Thankfully, someone had kept the area clear for the ceremony.

Willy met me in the parking lot with a smile on his face. "You ready for this, Boss? Gonna be bigger than you thought."

"Where are all these guys from?"

"Apparently Smitty posted it and guys from all over the state will be here."

"Will be?" I arched a brow.

"Yea, all over, Boss." He smiled again. "Looks like this will be one helluva party."

"Well, you and Dough Boy get on out of here and get more beer, booze, and food." I handed him the wad of cash in my pocket that totaled $1,200. "And be back here in two hours. I don't want to be worrying about my best man not showing up."

He rounded up Dough Boy and they headed into town in our van. Two hours later they returned with everything and got it set up. I passed the time greeting our unexpected guests and having a few beers. Not too many. I wanted to be able to recite my vows without stuttering or stumbling through the words.

Thirty minutes before the wedding, while I stood off to the side of the arbor, I got a text from Smitty that read: *Wish I could be there. You've done good with her. Treat her right or I'll kick your ass.*

I texted back: *You'll need an army to kick my ass.*

His reply said simply: *Now this is in the books, get ready to get patched in six weeks at the regional event.*

I smiled and looked up to see Sissy coming out of the clubhouse in her wedding dress. I choked back tears.

Chapter 6

Do You Smell......Blueberry Muffins?

In the few weeks between the wedding and the regional I dealt with more trouble than I had in the first nine months of being undercover. First, the bar was sucking us dry. We made money when we first opened, but after the initial honeymoon, things went south in a hurry. The fire marshal visited about every other week. Our customer base seemed to shrink. Inventory came up missing. Customers were breaking stuff behind our back. Just about every nightmare a bar owner could face, we faced. One of our girls got busted for prostitution—in the bar. She worked her regular shift on Friday night and about 11:00 p.m. we see this cop hauling her through the bar in handcuffs.

I hustled out from behind the bar and met them at the door. "What's going on, officer?"

While just about everyone in the bar watched our exchange, he explained that she offered her services, led him into the bathroom, and he arrested her when she took the agreed-upon fee.

"Way to get yourself busted," I said to her.

"I didn't know he was vice."

"Well, now you do."

She kicked at me. "I should spit on your face."

"Go for it." I eyed the cop. "What can you get her for if she spits in my face?" He pushed her toward the door and I opened it for him.

"So I guess you won't be bailing me out," she said.

"Not in a million years, sweetheart." While I headed to the bar, three couples stood to leave. I yelled, "Next round's on the house." They all sat down.

The little incident made the front page of the newspaper the next day. That hurt business in two ways. Her johns quit coming to the bar and regular folks didn't want to take a chance of getting caught up in a sting. I can't say that I blame them. If I were in their shoes, I'd probably have stopped too. I can't imagine how tough it might be to talk your way out of a prostitution sting when you didn't do anything wrong. I imagine a lot of marriages have taken a beating over the years because an innocent guy was nabbed for being in the wrong place at the wrong time.

Sissy and I sat down for dinner at our house about a week after the incident to discuss the future for the bar. After she set our dinner of meatloaf, mashed potatoes and green beans on the table, I prayed for our meal and thanked the Lord again for our safety. Some days we needed more protection than others. Today was certainly one of those days.

Goat, Old Man, and me rode out to see Willy at his shop. I had a miss in my engine. I could hear it, but it didn't seem to affect my power much. We had a long run coming up, about 3,000 miles in four days to visit clubs we needed to see before we got patched. Willy was busy working on a 454 for a 1973 Chevy Chevelle and didn't see us when we came in.

"Watch this," I said, sneaking up the side of the car.

Willy had practically crawled into the engine compartment. I grabbed him hard on the back of the leg and barked like a dog. He dropped a wrench and it clattered underneath the car. A few unintelligible words escaped his lips. He hit his head on the hood and then said a nice long string of intelligible cuss words. Of course, we laughed. He took a swing at me and then I reminded him, "You only swing when I swing." Rubbing his head, he did laugh at that one.

On the way back to the clubhouse, we stopped at a large discount store. After we dismounted, an old Cadillac Eldorado clipped Old Man's bike and drove off. Goat took off after the car and caught it at a stop sign at the end of the parking lot. Goat jumped off his bike and jammed a gun into the window. Much to his surprise, a little old man with a dirty white fedora sat staring back at him. Tears ran down the guy's face.

I pulled up a second later to hear Goat yell, "Do you know what you just did?"

The guy shook his head.

"You just hit my brother's bike."

"I'm, I'm, sorry, sorry," he said. "Was he hurt?"

Goat seemed a little flustered at this point. I think he expected to go batshit crazy on the oldster. "No, no he wasn't, but you just ruined his bike."

More tears streaked down the guy's face.

"He hit Old Man's bike?" Sissy asked.

"It was the damndest thing I've ever seen. I can't believe that Goat caught the guy and got him to come back."

"What happened then?"

"The guy followed Goat back up to where Old Man was and apologized. He even got out of his car and hugged Old Man." I chuckled. "I wish I had a camera for that one."

"Me too. Old Man doesn't like anyone to touch him."

That incident truly was one of the craziest things I'd ever seen, not just as a biker, but also in my entire life. I really thought Goat was gonna kill the guy when he got to the car. I thought for a second that the old man was acting to diffuse the situation. After a few minutes I could tell that he really was concerned about Old Man and didn't know that he had hit the bike. When he drove away the second time, he kept checking to make sure he didn't hit any of our bikes.

"We need to get rid of the bar," Sissy said with a touch of sadness in her voice.

"It's okay honey." I reached for her hand and she placed it in mine. "The bar's driving you crazy right now. You're always tired and never happy. It's not worth it."

"I feel like a failure." Her voiced quivered.

"You're not a failure."

"I love that place and our regulars."

"Everything has a time and season," I said trying to comfort her. "And it looks like that season is over."

"But it just started."

"Some seasons are shorter than others."

"I wish being undercover would be a shorter season."

I couldn't argue with that. The more the Feds pushed me to go deeper, the more strain it put on Sissy and me. She was fried, and I could tell. Whenever I was at the club, she made sure that she was with me. Not that she didn't trust me, but to keep women off me that were there to sleep with a biker. Plenty of women like that came around, and despite a number of options for them, some made it a sport to tag the boss. One chick that came to the clubhouse made it a point to announce she'd been with all but five bosses in the entire state. That's certainly not something I'd brag about. Between one-percent clubs and support clubs like us, we had 115 chapters in the state. But she wore that distinction like a badge of honor.

She is someone who could have benefitted from someone sharing the gospel with her. But Sissy and I had to keep our mouths shut.

"Do you want to close the bar or sell it to someone?" I asked between bites of potatoes.

"Let's see if we can sell it to Bender. I know his mother is sick and that is eating up a lot of his time, but maybe he'll take it."

"We probably won't make a profit."

"I don't care," she said. "I just want to get rid of it. It's sucking us dry right now."

"You know Ramey and Hector wanted to get in on the bar when we first opened. I'll see if we can figure something out and let them take over."

Life was pretty hectic at the moment. It seemed every night someone was on the verge of cutting someone, or smashing someone over the head with a beer bottle, or throwing someone through a window. I cried out many times in my spirit for one day of peace. Then it became one hour of peace. Then it was a prayer for one minute of peace.

Through it all, I leaned on the Lord for my peace of mind. I knew at some point we'd get what the Feds needed and we'd be done. When I pressed for an exit strategy, they never seemed to have one. The response was, "We need one more deal. We don't have enough."

One time Sissy and I went away for the weekend and the guys found us at a resort a couple of hours away. "How the heck did you find us?" I asked Willy while we lounged around the pool. That in and of itself was funny. Bikers drinking beer got a lot of nervous looks. We were so used to it at this point that we just laughed it off. Willy and me weren't in bad shape, but some of the guys had guts that were just flat out gross.

At the Valentine's Day bash, a beer company sponsored a "Biggest Beer Belly" contest for men and women. That was just downright disgusting. For nearly an hour, two young chicks in black swimwear and high heels measured the biggest and worst bellies. I don't remember the winning measurement for the women. The guy who won measured eighty-three inches. That's one big gut.

When we went back up to the room, someone had lit up, which wasn't surprising. A couple of the guys smoked more weed than humanly possible. Sissy was pinned in the back and motioned for me.

"You have got to get me out of here," she said. "I'm getting sick from all this pot."

"Smells like blueberry muffins," I said.

"Not funny." She slapped me on the arm. "Seriously, I need to get out of here or I'm gonna be sick."

I made an excuse to leave and pulled Sissy from the mob of women who surrounded her.

"I wanna come too," Goat's girlfriend Jersey said.

"You guys stay here and enjoy the room," Sissy said. "I need some alone time with my man. We'll be back in a little bit."

We went out to the bike and acted like we were getting something out of the saddlebags. I lit up a cigarette while Sissy faked it. Sissy pulled out her phone.

"Who are you calling?"

"Ramey."

I took the phone from her. "Not here. Someone could walk up."

"They are twenty bikers in that suite right now. There's enough dope and pot in that room right now to wrap up this case."

"They're not gonna do anything. That's not what they're after." I could see she was about to crack. I threw my butt on the ground and pulled her close.

"I'm not sure how much longer I can do this."

"It won't be much longer," I said, stroking her hair. "After we patch, we'll be about done."

"Ah, isn't that nice," a female voice said behind me.

"Jersey, go away," Sissy said, pulling away from me.

"But you left right in the middle of our conversation."

Still holding Sissy, I turned. "Give us a minute and we'll be back up."

We watched her wobble away on her high heels.

"That was close," I said. "If you'd been on the phone she would have caught us."

Before she answered, I heard what sounded like a gunshot near the pool area. *Oh God*, I thought, *I hope one of my guys didn't just shoot someone.* Then I heard two guys yelling and a woman shrieking. *Crap, that's what happened*, I thought. Sissy and I took off running across the parking lot. I did my best to keep hold of her hand until she let go.

93

"Go, I'll catch up," she said.

The intensity of the shouting match grew as I got closer and I could see Chicken had Smoke bent backwards over the hood of car with a knife on him. Another guy, Tiny, was off to the side encouraging Chicken. Tiny had a hammer in his hand.

Still running, I yelled, "Stand down." No one listened and I yelled again. This time I got a response.

"You stay out of this, Boss," said Tiny.

I stopped next to the fender of the car. "What's going on here, boys?"

"This is between me and Smoke," said Chicken, who outweighed Smoke by about eighty pounds and had no trouble keeping him pinned on the car. "I caught him stealing money from my wallet."

"Is that true?" I said to Smoke.

Smoke shook his head.

A crowd had started to gather on the other side of the fence, mostly little kids who are usually more curious than the adults. I needed to diffuse this quickly or Chicken might just kill Smoke. "Let him up."

"But—"

"You guys know better," I said. "You need to take that up on your own. We don't put laundry out here."

Chicken let go of Smoke.

I relaxed for the first time since arriving at the car. "Are we done?" When no one answered, I repeated the question.

94

All three answered in unison in what sounded like a poorly planned musical. Chicken had a deep, booming response, Tiny was high-pitched, and Smoke was still trying to catch his breath.

"Well then, get on out of here. Sissy and I came up here for some peace and quiet. Now that you've ruined that, take your crap home, and we'll settle this at the clubhouse when we get back."

Chicken started to say something and I held up my hand.

"Understood?"

They nodded.

"Before you go, I'm fining each of you $100."

"I don't have it on me," Smoke said.

"Then give me the keys to your bike."

"But—"

"But nothing. You borrow the money or give me the keys."

Sure enough, Smoke asked Chicken for the money and Chicken gave it to him. After they left, I said to Sissy, "One of these days that's gonna go real bad and we'll end up in prison for a long time."

Chapter 7

Love, Loyalty, and Respect

A few days before the regional event, Smitty called to see what I was doing. It was 11:00 p.m. and I was hanging out at the bar. Despite wanting to get rid of it, we hadn't found a buyer and it looked like we just might have to shut down. We really didn't want to go that route, but if no one stepped up soon that's what we'd have to do. We'd take a beating financially, even if we sold off any equipment that we could.

When I told Smitty where I was, he said, "You need to be at the club hanging with your boys. Besides, you need to just burn that place down and collect the insurance money."

That thought had crossed my mind. But I couldn't bring myself to do it. I knew what Proverbs 14:23 says, "All hard work brings a profit, but mere talk leads only to poverty."

"If you don't want to do it that way, tick off that rival gang of yours and hope they fire bomb the place."

Now, that was a thought that hadn't crossed my mind. But I dismissed it quickly. "I can't do that. There's too many other businesses connected to this one. I don't want someone else to lose their business."

"Bah," Smitty said. "You're talking like a Bible-thumping hard head. Think like a biker, man. Think like a biker." Then he cackled.

That cackle told me he'd been drinking. "Where are you?"

"At your clubhouse. Now get up here. We need to talk."

I gave instructions to our bartender to close up at the normal time, 2:00 a.m., and I arrived at the clubhouse about fifteen minutes later. Smitty greeted me on his bike when I rolled through the gate.

"Follow me," he said.

When a guy in Smitty's position gives an order, you just follow. You don't ask questions. You just go. He led me out of town. What a beautiful night to ride. The wind whipped through my hair. We rode for about forty minutes on roads that I'd never been. When we finally stopped, I had no idea where we were.

"Follow me," Smitty said when we dismounted.

This was getting a little creepy as he led me up a trail to the top of a small mountain. The moon was full so we didn't need flashlights to navigate the trail. I didn't ask any questions and he walked and I kept following. Finally we reached the top. We could hear wildlife skittering away into the bushes near the trail. One time I stepped on a snake when I thought it was a twig. That's never a comfortable feeling with all the rattlesnakes in the area. When we reached the top, Smitty looked up into

97

the heavens. For a minute I thought he might be praying. I walked a few steps away to give him some privacy.

"Come back here."

When I did, he said, "Take a deep breath."

I inhaled sweet, cool air. I filled my lungs and held it.

"Smell that?"

I didn't smell anything so I took another breath. He noticed.

"You don't, do you."

I looked him in the eye, and answered that I didn't.

"Take another breath and I'll tell you what you smell."

I inhaled deeper than before, still hoping to smell what he did.

"Freedom, son." I looked at him with what must have been a weird look. "That's what you smell, and don't look at me that way."

I laughed and reached for a pack of cigarettes in my vest. I pulled out one and handed it to Smitty, and I tapped one out for myself.

"You'll never have it this easy again. When you patch, some of the guys in your club will change. They won't blindly follow you like they do now." He paused to pull in a long drag. The embers on the end burned bright. "They'll challenge you more, stand up to you more, even question your authority. Loyalty fades away and pride starts to shine through."

"You always told me that the patch doesn't make the man, the man makes the patch and it's easier to get than it is to keep. So if that starts to happen we will just have to start weedin' 'em out. I just hope I can ride as hard as you do thirty years from now."

Deep down I would really love to be riding thirty years from now but I know that isn't in God's plan for me. I loved that old man. Honestly, loved him.

I finished my cigarette and crushed my butt on the ground.

"So enjoy it. It's all about to change."

I appreciated that Smitty looked out for me. I know he felt I was always there for him. And I was. But he also was always there for me, and not just for club matters. That man had a lot of wisdom and some people were too proud to tap into that wisdom.

"I love this place," he said, breaking into my thoughts.

"How's come?"

He pointed to a spot in the darkness that I couldn't see. "Right over there, I drank my first beer." He pivoted and faced the opposite direction. "Over there I got some for the first time. The same night I smoked weed for the first time."

"Why are they in different spots?"

"I drank the beer with my dad while on a trip with him when I was thirteen. We used to camp up here a lot when I was a kid. When I was fifteen, I brought the weed and the girl up here alone."

He seemed to ponder the memories of those incidents. He didn't speak for the longest time. A breeze had picked up and I rubbed my arm to create warmth. Finally, he spoke. "You know I didn't bring you up here away from Sissy and everyone else to tell you about my first beer and weed."

"And girl," I added.

"That too." He laughed. "I brought you up here to give you something." Then he punched me in the gut.

I stumbled backward, trying to catch my breath and not lose my footing at the same time. When I could get air into my lungs again, I asked, "You can't be serious."

He let out that cackle again. I'm sure the coyotes and other wildlife nearby took off running. "Stand up. I do have something I want to give you." He reached inside his shirt and pulled out a necklace and unclasped it. "Here," he said, dropping it into my hand.

"What is it?"

"A one-percenter necklace that was given to me by the brother who patched me in years ago." He wiped at his face. "I want you to have it."

"Why?"

"You ask a lot of questions, you know that?"

"Inquiring minds want to know."

"You want me to punch you in the gut again?

"Now *you're* asking a lot of questions."

He faked a punch to the gut. I didn't flinch.

"That's my boy." He smiled as I started to put on the necklace. "You can't let anyone see it until after you guys patch. Tiger won't like that I gave it to you before. Plus, I think he wants it. As far as we know, it's one of the first necklaces like this ever made."

"I thought we got rings."

"That's the new way. Back in the day we did the necklace, like dog tags, you know. But too many guys got 'em yanked off in a fight, either at a bar or by their old lady. So we switched to rings. Which was a good move because you could hurt someone with one."

I dropped the necklace into a safe pocket inside my cut, near where I kept my private recorder. I didn't know what to say. I knew Smitty thought a lot of me, but this was something else. Much more than I realized.

"You're a good kid," he said, patting me on the face. "You're doing good as a leader, which I knew you would. Don't muck it up and treat that lady of yours right. Ya hear me?"

I nodded. The gentle part of me wanted to shed a tear. The believer part of me wanted to share the gospel with Smitty right there on the mountaintop. The caring side of me wanted to warn him that something serious was about to go down. But the biker side of me won out and I simply said, "I do."

"Let's get you back down the mountain to that woman of yours so she isn't worried that old Smitty has got you out whoring around."

I did my best to sneak into the bedroom without waking my bride. I failed.

She clicked on the light on the nightstand. "It's 3:00 a.m."

101

"I know."

"You could have called or texted me."

"I thought you knew I was with Smitty."

"I did, but I didn't know where."

"We ended up on some mountain that he went to a lot as a kid."

"Oh, that's nice."

I understood her anger. I would've been mad if I was in her shoes but I wanted to change the subject. And quick. "You'll never believe what happened on the mountain."

"Can't it wait until morning?"

I dropped the necklace into her hand.

"What's this?"

"Look at it."

Her eyes widened. "Is this what I think it is?"

"Yes. Smitty gave it to me."

"This looks old."

"It is. He got it when he patched."

She handed the necklace back to me. "You need to wash that thing before you wear it. Who knows where that thing has been."

I crawled into bed. "You're such a girl."

Everyone in the club was pretty jacked up the morning we left for the regional event near Las Vegas. That was a quick trip for us, about four hours. That wasn't bad considering the number of miles we rode the last few months. During one four-day stretch, we covered 6,000 miles.

That was an insane four days. We'd get to a club to introduce ourselves to drum up support and stay for a couple of hours and then be back on the road. One stop, we stayed thirty minutes, drank a quick beer, and took off. Thank goodness we had good weather. Running that many miles in rain would have been disastrous. Today was another good day to ride. Clear blue skies that we get often in the west and air free of smog.

A nervous energy permeated throughout the club grounds as we got ready. This was a big day for us. We were moving up from a support club to a one-percent club. I stood on the porch and watched the guys— Dough Boy, Dick, Trent, Old Man, Willy, Spade and a few others—load up their saddlebags. The property girls were busy inside.

I checked my watch. "Thirty minutes, boys."

Old Man came up on the porch and stood next to me. "You don't seem nervous about any of this."

"No reason to be." I smiled. "Isn't this what we're made for? Isn't this supposed to be our lot in life?"

"The baddest of the bad," he added.

"You know how corny that sounds?"

"Well yeah, but it's true." He turned and walked inside.

And he was right. Bikers want to be perceived as the baddest of the bad, and probably every other cliché on the planet. I loved being part of a group of guys who genuinely loved each other. I've seen one guy pull on another guy and threaten to kill him. Then an hour later they'd be at the bar having a beer and laughing about it. Most people probably don't get that. People in the "real" world like to hold grudges. We don't have time for that in a motorcycle club. We have to have each other's back because no one else will. If a gang rolled into town and got into a fight, do you think the president of the bank would have our back? No, more than likely he'd be one of the first people calling the cops on us.

When it was time, I ordered everyone to line up. Yes, we had a formation that we rode in. Being the highest-ranking officer, I rode left front. The other officers filled in according to their role in the club. After that, guys took a spot with the probates in the back. One full patch took the rear. I fired up the bike and Sissy climbed onto the back. She whispered that she loved me and I patted her on the leg. I led the way out of the grounds.

A myriad of emotions took turns dominating my thoughts as we headed toward Vegas. I thought about how God had orchestrated getting patched sooner than the normal year. I thought about the case, about how it had mushroomed since we went in and how the Feds kept pushing for more information on more people. I thought about Sissy and how losing the bar bothered her, how she was holding up while being undercover, and how she handled being a new bride. As if on cue, she gave me a squeeze around my waist.

Halfway to Vegas, we stopped to get gas at one of those places with vintage pumps and the stereotypical grease monkey sitting in a rocker by the front door. I didn't think those places really existed. I gassed up first and while the others took turns, I checked my cell. Smitty had called about forty minutes ago.

When I called he didn't bother with a greeting. "You got a choice to make, boy."

"What are you talking about?"

"Stop with the questions."

"Well, tell me what choices I have to make."

"I'm not at the regional. You can go up there and hang with those hoodlums or you can come hang with me."

"Where are—"

"I'm in a little motel about eighty miles north of Vegas on U.S. 93. You've got to sundown to make your choice," he added and clicked off.

I didn't know what to say. It seemed that everything was about to come unraveled. I kicked at an imaginary pebble.

"What's wrong?" Sissy asked as she walked up from behind.

"Something's up and I don't know what it is." I recounted the conversation with Smitty.

"What are you going to do?"

"I don't know. I can't back out on Smitty, but we need to patch. Everything could fall apart if we don't." I kicked at a real pebble this time and it skidded to a stop near the gas pumps. "I don't have to decide right now."

Hours later, after we rolled through Vegas, we rode up on Interstate 15 toward the regional. Exit signs for U.S. 93 appeared and I knew I had to choose: straight for the regional or left, toward Smitty.

I chose left and an unknown future.

Chapter 8

Friends, Foes, and Family

We found Smitty at some little motel nestled up against the base of a mountain range, one of those places whose vacancy sign has a missing letter or two. Smitty was in his room alone. We didn't expect anything else, but it saddened me to see my boss cower in a little rat hole like this all by himself. A guy like him didn't deserve to be disrespected like he was.

All twenty of us jammed into this little tiny hotel room and listened to Smitty explain that Tiger was not happy about us getting patched just six months after becoming a support club. The rule is one year, and we were blowing that out of the water in a huge way. Smitty didn't want a big showdown with Tiger at the regional event. Of course, we were disappointed that we weren't getting patched, but we also had looked forward to some of the other events.

The biggest beer belly contest was gaining popularity and rumor had it someone with a ninety-two-inch waist planned to enter. Of course, the popular bikini and wet T-shirt contests were scheduled as well as the dunk tank, the game with the chicken and a bingo card, a chili cook-off and other stuff for adults. The kids stuff included ring toss, bucket ball, beanbag toss and shooting gallery game in which the guns spray water.

And for the first time, a swap meet was being held at the regional event. That would have been cool to see. Swap meets were usually held separately, but in another move to assert himself, Tiger instructed Splash to include a swap meet.

At a swap meet, vendors and bikers bring in accessories, bike parts, etc. One can find complete bikes, front ends, handlebars, you name it. If it is part of a bike or a bike accessory, like a new or vintage jacket, you can find it at a swap meet. Shopping on the Internet is great, but some guys like me need to feel, see, and touch the merchandise. Swap meets are interactive. Haggling is very much a part of the experience.

Swap meets will vary in size, but three things are common at each: parts, big selection, and great deals. Swap meets are a mixture of treasure hunting and shopping, sort of like garage sales. Some flock to the meets to search for hidden jewels amongst the used and antique parts, spending hours sifting through bins and turning over chrome on the vendor tables. Others just want to check the latest accessories or models. Some guys—Willy, for instance—take stuff that has accumulated in their garage with the hope of making a little bit of money.

Also for the first time ever, a Harley V-Rod Muscle was up for silent auction. When I heard, I called Ramey and said that I wanted some money from the Feds so I could bid on the bike. He didn't think that was funny and replied with an emphatic "no."

I didn't barter or buy much at the swap meets, but I enjoyed walking around with Sissy and checking out all the cool stuff that vendors and other bikers brought. I remember one time I saw a helmet shaped into the mask of the alien from the *Predator* movies. I spent about an hour with that guy. His work was phenomenal. He said he spent about 150 hours getting the helmet just right with dreadlocks and all. He let me try it on, and he even had the special lens for the eyes. Pretty cool, to say the least. I don't remember how much he wanted for the helmet, but it was more than I wanted to pay.

I often sought out specially designed and painted gas tanks. I had to catch myself a couple of times when I found myself gazing at tanks that sported a cross with the sun behind it, or Christ hanging on the cross. Most of the time I'd glance at the work, compliment the artist if he was there, and then move on. This one bike, though, I had to stay and admire. The artist had painted an overhead view of Christ on the cross. All you could see was the top of Christ's head with the crown of thorns and the top of the cross with the Hebrew, Latin and Greek words for: *Jesus of Nazareth, the King of the Jews.* Amazing. I couldn't get over the detail and how the artist brought the artwork to life. I cried. Sissy saw this and told me to get it together. "I can't help it," I said. The rest

109

of the bike, a black low rider, was covered in patches of thorns similar to what was placed on Christ's head. One of my guys came over while Sissy and I were admiring the bike. He glanced at it and said, "Only a fool would believe in a God who allows the pain and suffering we see in the world." He walked off and my heart hurt a little more for him.

I got to know the artist a little bit at that meet. He wasn't a believer, but I still hoped to see him again. Now that wasn't going to happen.

With all of us crammed into his room, Smitty outlined his plan to get us patched. Some of the guys were not happy, Old Man in particular. Getting patched meant a lot to guys like him. Not only was being in the club important, he didn't have much of a home life. That patch was a badge of honor for him. And others too. Trent was unhappy about the delay, but didn't say much. Later, when we both stepped outside for some fresh air and a smoke, I asked. "What's bugging you?"

"Nothing."

"Are you hiding something from me?"

He shook his head. "You know I'm always straight with you, no matter what it is."

"I know you are. But I had to ask."

"And I always tell you." He smiled.

"So, why do you seem so down about not getting patched this weekend?" We both lit up at the same time.

"I've never really belonged to anything before."

"You belong now," I said.

"Not really," he said. "We're a support group for The Forsaken Ones. We're not our own group."

I could see where he was going with this. His attitude really wasn't uncommon for guys in a support club. Oftentimes they feel less than equal. These guys long for the equal footing of being a "real" chapter, although the only thing that really changes is the patch and the name. It's still the same guy and the same clubhouse. The same old ladies. The same bikes. We don't get upgrades on any of those things.

"We will be, don't worry." I patted him on the shoulder. "Smitty's got a plan that will work."

He didn't seem to hear me. "You know, when I was in high school, I was the kid who sat in the back of every class. I wore my leather jacket everywhere. I was the guy who listened to Motley Crue, Ratt, Ozzy, KISS, and Def Leppard when everyone was listening to Nirvana and Pearl Jam. I never fit in." He looked off toward the hills behind the motel. "Never."

"None of us did," I said, trying to reassure him. God, I wanted to share the gospel with him. He thought belonging to a "real" bike club would solve all his problems. I knew it wouldn't and it killed me inside to know that truth and not be able to tell him. Not just the truth about how life as a biker could be the death of him. But the truth of Jesus Christ, the reason we all have been saved from our sin and wretched ways.

I pulled a loogey from my sinuses and let it fly about eight feet away.

"Good one, Boss," he said with a snicker.

"Let me tell you a story about myself."

His snicker turned into a chuckle. "You getting all sappy on me here?"

"No, but I think you'll understand something when I share this."

"What's that?"

"You'll see." And then I danced a fine line between this temporal world and the heavenly realm. I was careful not to downplay his thoughts and ideas that being a biker was the end-all and be-all of life. I carefully danced around that issue and pointed out there can be more to life than just "belonging." I shared that we all have a purpose and mission in life. The key is to find that mission, whatever that may be, and then to live with purpose to fulfill that mission.

He looked at me, his eyebrows scrunched together. "What if I think my mission is to be a lifelong biker?"

"It very well could be." I threw my butt on the sidewalk and crushed it out.

"But what if I discovered that it's not?"

"Then you keep looking for as long as it takes."

"I hope it doesn't take long. I think a lifetime of seeking might be exhausting."

"It can be, but when you find it, life just falls into place."

112

"How do you know that you've found yours? Not everything seems like it has fallen in place for you. The bar is going under and we're not getting patched this weekend."

"That doesn't mean I haven't found my mission and purpose. When you do, you're not promised a lifetime of easy going. Things will still be tough at times. And when they are, that's when you build character."

"You sound like my old man." He threw his butt on the ground and crushed it with his boot. "He was always yelling about getting my crap together and making something of myself."

"What does he say about you being in a biker club?"

"He doesn't know," A strange look came over this face. "He died about three years ago of a heart attack."

"Sorry, man. I shouldn't—"

"You didn't know." He wiped his nose with the back of his hand.

"What would he say if he was still alive?"

"That this isn't it."

"What do you think?"

"I think it is. I think this is my, what did you call it?"

"Your mission and purpose."

"Yea. That." He sniffled. "Is it possible that it's not?"

Man, he was so close. So close that all I had to do was say the word. But I couldn't. I would have blown up the whole case. At that moment, I wanted to take off my cut and throw it on the ground and quit

113

the case. I felt like I was renouncing my faith in Christ. A lump formed in my throat. I said a quick, silent prayer for the right words. And they came instantly.

"For months, I've been trying to come up with the right nickname for you. I think I finally have found one."

He glanced at me; his eyes wet with unshed tears and a look of expectation.

"I'm gonna call you Seeker from now on."

He fixed his gaze on the ground and nodded his head slightly a few times before speaking. "I like that." He looked up at me. "It fits."

Along with not being able to share my faith during this ordeal, losing my family hurt almost as much. Sissy and I both had to sever ties with parents, siblings, aunts, uncles, cousins, nieces, and nephews. It was brutal. We tried to explain to a couple of them, but they didn't get it. They pleaded with us to change our minds, and when we wouldn't they wanted to stay in touch. We couldn't risk the chance of them saying or doing something that might blow the case. We also couldn't stay in touch because of their safety. That part I think some of them got.

Not being with our family members was especially tough at birthdays, Thanksgiving, and Christmas. And none of them could attend our wedding. That hurt. A lot. Our families, particularly our parents, didn't get to see my beautiful bride.

When she walked out of the clubhouse that day I choked back tears. A friend from the old days told me that when he and his wife got married, he almost hyperventilated when he saw her at the back of the church. When she got to the altar, she looked at him, all white and struggling to breathe. She thought he was having second thoughts and wanted to back out. When she asked him that question, he couldn't answer. She got mad, stormed back down the aisle, and fled outside. After he recovered, he went outside and explained the situation. Relieved, she entered the church with him. They'd been married nine years at the time he told me the story.

When I saw Sissy that night, I understood what he went through. She was gorgeous in her gown with thin straps, a tight-fitting torso with thin white braided V-neck that plunged down her back to a large lace tie bow. Her dress puffed out slightly all the way down to a one-foot round even train. She wore a shorter veil that stopped just above her chest.

And not a single person from our families was in attendance. That still bothered me.

Two instances really tore us up when it came to family. For Sissy, she had been really close with a young niece. Sissy tried to explain what was about to happen, but the little girl didn't understand. We found out later that the girl thought Sissy had abandoned her. She couldn't understand that Sissy needed to go away for a little while with Uncle Boss to take care of some business. It took some time for the two to rebuild that relationship.

I had a nephew that needed help while we were in and I couldn't do anything. Dope has been a problem for my sister all her life. She never married and had a child out of wedlock. That tore up my mother. She got busted about three months after we went in, and it looked like the state would take her kid. I about lost it. I couldn't let him go to the state. I went to Ramey and Hector for help. Ramey brought up the fact that I didn't have a job, the bar notwithstanding, and I was considered a terrorist.

"We can't do anything," Ramey said. "Our hands are tied."

"There's gotta be something we can do. That kid will end up in the state's hands and who knows what will happen then?"

"You have to trust everything will work out just fine," Hector said.

Trust. That wasn't a foreign concept to me. Trust in God is one thing, but trust in the state system was another. I fumed for days over that conversation. I couldn't believe that Feds would let something like that happen to a little child. My nephew was nine at the time.

One morning at breakfast I read a scripture that changed my attitude about the situation. Psalm 18:30-31 reads, "As for God, his way is perfect: The Lord's word is flawless; he shields all who take refuge in him."

After that I turned it over to God that he would take care of my nephew and everything would be fine.

Being tied up in knots is not something I enjoy. I can't imagine anyone does. Being undercover in situations and places that could erupt into a violent or deadly outbreak in an instance take a strong-minded person to handle. And it seemed the cracks in Sissy's makeup were growing bigger every day. At night, she'd toss and turn while having nightmares. Her demeanor changed too. Her sassy tone, which was one of the early attractions, became a bitter tone. She often snapped at people at the bar, even customers, and at the club. And everyone noticed. Dough Boy came up to me one night at the clubhouse after Sissy barked at him while serving his dinner.

"That old lady of yours is getting out of hand," he said.

"She's just having a hard time dealing with closing the bar."

"Nah, man. It's more than that." He took a bite of food. "She's getting mean and sniping at everything." He shoveled in another bite. "And some of us are getting tired of it. My old lady is about to punch her lights out."

"I'll talk to her about it."

With a half plate of food, he got up and left the table.

That night I brought it up with Sissy when we got home. And I brought it up gently while we got ready for bed. When I did, she struck like a rattlesnake. Her tirade lasted a good thirty minutes.

"Can't you see I'm about to crack?" she said at one point. "And you're not doing anything about it. You just go around taking care of your boys and don't care one iota about me." A few minutes later she ripped off a good one, "I'd like to see Ramey and Hector do what we do. They couldn't handle it. I know I shouldn't be bashing them, but I'm getting tired of them pushing us to do more and more and more."

117

I wanted to interject, but knew better than to jump in at this point. She was on a roll and I needed her to flame out before I said anything. Finally, I got my chance. "What is it you want me to do?"

"Don't play that with me," she said, her eyes blazing. "You need to figure out what you need to do to fix this. I'm not telling you. If you don't know by now …"

I held her as she started to sob. We rocked in unison for a while as I realized this was a lose-lose situation for us. And somehow we needed to find a way to win. Or I was about to lose my wife.

Chapter 9

A Birthday Hit

Life was coming unraveled in a hurry. We didn't patch the weekend of the regional and Smitty's plan to patch us the following weekend didn't happen either because he got hurt working at his club and ended up on crutches.

In the meantime, we sold the bar to a local guy who had a connection with strip clubs in Phoenix. A rumor floated around for weeks that we would turn the bar into a strip club. Fortunately for the locals, that didn't happen. The new owner reopened as a bar with a new name and under new management. People flocked to the place, just like they had when we opened.

Needless to say, morale among my boys was pretty low at this point. I think I had to break up more fights at the club than ever before. Willy got into it with Dough Boy. Seeker got into it with Old Man. Dough Boy got into it with me. Spade fought Seeker. And Chief, my treasurer who was usually pretty quiet, duked it out with Willy. This all took place in the first week. I was about to lose my mind. Like Sissy, I wasn't sure how much longer I could take this. I laid awake many nights pleading with God to bring a quick end to it.

Two weeks after Smitty got hurt, Dough Boy told me he heard about a hit on me. I can't say I was surprised. This stuff happens all the time in biker clubs. In prison I had guys gunning for me too. So this wasn't new to me. Playing the role to the hilt, I said to Dough Boy, "If there really is a hit on me, bring me the guy running his mouth."

Two days later I was behind the bar grabbing a beer when Dough Boy hauled this fat drunk (who looked like he hadn't shaved or showered in a month) into the clubhouse.

"Take him outside and hose him off," I said, getting off the bar stool where I sat nursing a beer. "I don't want that stink in my clubhouse." When I was about to call Sissy and then Ramey, Old Man came in escorting a chick in high heels, a short leather skirt, and tank top. She, too, looked like she hadn't bathed in a week, her blonde hair matted against her head and eyeliner applied a little too heavy.

"We brought 'em in the cage," Old Man said, referring to the van.

"Hose her off too."

"Gladly."

I thought I caught a smile when he turned to take her outside. The phone in my hand rang. Caller ID showed Sissy. I snapped open the phone. "You need to get here right away."

"Thanks for the warm greeting."

"Blame it on Red. I learned it from him."

"Well, you wait till I see him next time. Did you–"

"Seriously, I need you to get down here right away. And call Ramey on your way. Something serious is about to go down and it could be bad."

"Are you in danger?"

"I might be. Dough Boy…" I paused when I saw the man I was about to speak of was pushed, the guy stripped down to his shorts, through the front door. "…And if you could pick up some lunch meat and a loaf of bread. Oh, I think we're out of mustard too."

"Are you on crack?"

"Is Sissy getting food?" Dough Boy asked.

I nodded. "And Dough Boy wants three tacos from that place down the street that he likes." I whispered, "Get here quick." Then louder, "Love you."

Dough Boy opened his mouth to make a smartass comment but I held up my hand to stop. "You don't need to bust my chops about telling Sissy that I love her. One of these days when you have an old lady that you're willing to keep, you'll tell her you love her too." I looked at the soaking wet fat man dripping water all over my clubhouse. "What's your name?"

When he didn't answer, Dough Boy gave him a good shake.

"Tree."

Dough Boy and I laughed. This guy looked no more like a tree than I do a saint. "I think I'll call you twig instead. Is that okay with you?"

"You wouldn't call him that if you saw what was between his legs," the woman blurted as Old Man shoved her inside.

"Is that why you can't walk straight?"

"Asshole," was her reply.

"Put her on the couch and don't let her open her mouth."

I looked at the guy again. "I don't suppose I need to search you, do I?"

He shook his head, and it looked like he had a new welt on his left check. Dough Boy kept his arms pinned behind him. *Sissy, where the hell are you?* I thought. *I need you here.* I heard a car door and Sissy, out of breath, bolted into the clubhouse a few seconds later. Our eyes met. She looked scared to death. I didn't show that in my eyes, but I was inside.

"Watch her," I said, pointing to the woman Old Man was guarding. She too was stripped to her underwear. I now wished I wouldn't have had the boys hose her off. She looked much better with what little clothes she previously had on.

I started toward our private room and said, "Bring him."

I stepped aside while Dough Boy herded Tree into the room and Old Man followed. I reached up and touched the flag, stepped inside, and closed the door. I entered just as Dough Boy flung the guy into the couch along the opposite wall. Tree's head smacked the wall. *Good for Dough Boy*, I thought. *Being a man, finally.*

I started in on the guy right away. "What's this about a hit on me?"

Rubbing his head, Tree sat up. "I don't know much. I just heard some guy talking at the bar the other night."

"Our bar?"

"No, we were at Los Gatos. The old lady and me were having some beers with another couple and we overheard this guy talking about a hit on a bar owner. I went over to his table and asked why he was

122

running his mouth. He spit at me. So I punched him in the face and knocked him down. Then I picked him up off the floor. I asked him again why he was running his mouth. He said that he wanted the word to get back to you."

I walked over and got in his face. "You're a dead man if I find out you're lying."

"I'm not—"

Dough Boy kicked him. "Don't interrupt the man when he's talking."

"Like I was saying, you're a dead man if I find out you're lying. It didn't take us long to find you this time. And we'll find you again. Understand?" I backed up. "Now get out of here."

He bolted for the door and Old Man tripped him on the way out. Tree hit the edge of a couch by the door and slammed to the floor. We all laughed.

"Hurt yourself," Old Man said, laughing.

After Tree gathered up his woman, they ran outside, only to come back in wearing their stinking clothes. "We need a ride."

"Walk," I said, taking my place at the bar again.

At first, I was mad about the hit, but I couldn't show it. Not in front of the guys. As a chapter boss, you learned to live with it. If someone wanted your chapter, they'd put a hit out on you. Sometimes they succeeded. Sometimes they didn't. For Sissy and mine's sake, I hope they didn't this time.

They left without objecting. I turned to Dough Boy, who sat next to me. "What the hell is wrong with you? That's the wrong guy. I want the guy running his mouth, not the guy who heard the guy. Now go get me the guy who's running his mouth."

Dough Boy and Old Man left, leaving Sissy and me alone in the club. That didn't happen often.

"That girl is a piece of work," she said. "She is so strung out on meth right now that the bottom part of her mouth doesn't move. "I don't understand people who abuse their bodies like that."

For the next forty-five minutes we leaned against the bar and faced the front door. We talked about the case, possibly having kids, the relief of selling the bar until Seeker showed up.

"I just saw Dough Boy and Old Man getting tacos. Dough Boy's pretty pissed that Sissy didn't have tacos when she showed up."

I caught Sissy's eye and gave her a half-frown.

"Oh, crap," she said, "I'll never hear the end of it from that boy."

"Don't worry about him," I said. "And you did forget the lunch meat, bread, and mustard."

She headed toward the door.

"Love you," I said.

"Sure you do," she said, pushing open the door.

Seeker took Sissy's place against the bar. "I didn't want to say anything in front of her, but Dough Boy said there's a hit on you. Is that true?"

"They're looking for the guy who is spouting off at the mouth about it. When they bring him in, we'll get to the bottom of it. In the meantime, let's shoot some pool."

While we played, Seeker asked questions like, "Are you nervous?" "Will you kill the guy who's running his mouth?" "What if he kills you first?" After a few minutes of questions like that, I stepped away from the pool table and said, "How would you answer those questions?"

"I'd be nervous as shit, scared out of my pants, and hope the guy didn't kill me before I could kill him."

"You really could kill the guy?"

He pursed his lips and tightened his grip on his pool stick. "Of course. Gotta live by the saying, kill or be killed."

Satisfied with his answer, I bent over the cue ball to take my shot when Dough Boy brought in another guy. This guy was about the same size as Tree, but a lot more drunk.

"What's up sisters?" he said, slurring his words.

"Bring him," I said, starting for the private room and then to Seeker, "Coming?" I grabbed a hall full bottle of vodka from the bar.

He fell in line behind Dough Boy pushing the motor mouth, and Old Man. I touched the flag again and entered our private room. For the second time today, Dough Boy tossed a guy into the couch and he hit his head.

"Dang, don't be so rough," our visitor said.

125

"Shut up," I said. He started to open his mouth and I threw the bottle at him. I missed by about a foot to the left of his head. The bottle smashed against the wall, sending glass and booze all over the place. He suddenly sobered up and pulled. My boys pulled and I wielded the knife I told people I used for hunting. With his gun trained on us, I said to Dough Boy, "You didn't think to pat him down?"

"Sorry, Boss."

"A little late for that, don't you think?"

Mr. Suddenly Sober chimed in. "You guys gonna get it on or what?"

"The only person that I plan to get into it with is you."

He stood, his gun aimed at my chest.

"There's four of us and one of you. In what scenario do you think you get out of this alive?"

"Kill the head the body will die is what I heard. Maybe I should see if that's true." He cocked his revolver.

I didn't flinch. I couldn't. Not in front of my boys. "I really don't think you want to do that."

Dough Boy and Old Man took a step toward the guy. And Seeker, who had been standing behind me off to the left, flew past me and put his gun on the guy's temple. "I think you might want to reconsider that last statement."

While proud of Seeker for standing up for me, I was also a little scared too. The guy had started to shake and I was afraid that he might accidentally shoot me. I moved to the right to get out of his line of fire while Old Man reached over and took the guy's gun. I needed to relieve some pressure so I picked up a can of beer that sat on the table near me. Surprisingly it was full. I chucked it at the guy and I smacked him right in the face. The guy dropped like the proverbial sack of potatoes. The boys and me laughed.

Dough Boy pulled the guy to his feet and dropped him into the couch. Again. This time without smacking his head off the wall.

"Now that we have your attention," I said, while he looked up at me with blood trickling from his nose. "Who's got the hit out on me?"

"I dunno," he said.

"So why are you running around town telling people that there's a hit on me? That doesn't make sense."

With my knife still in my hand, I stepped around a table that sat in the middle of the room and pressed the edge against the side of his face. "Tell me who has the hit on me. You seriously can't be stupid enough to tell people without knowing who put out the hit."

"Splash." He tried to push away the knife, but I held it firm against his skull. "Splash ordered the hit."

"Why?"

"How should I know? I was at the clubhouse north of Phoenix and heard someone talking about it."

"So why are you hear shooting off your mouth?"

"I wanted to draw you out. For the reward."

"Fine job you did there. I've got you in my clubhouse with knife on your face and my boys with itchy trigger fingers. Good job."

This was getting to be too much. Way too much. Crap was starting to happen that I had no control over. I knew Sissy would freak when she heard about this. But I couldn't keep it from her. She was bound to hear it from someone else if I didn't tell her. Then she walked through the front door screaming my name.

"Keep 'em on him," I said to my boys and left the room.

"Why didn't you tell me?" She ran toward me with an arm full of groceries that she set on the counter and then punched me. "I can't believe that you didn't tell me." She kept hitting me and saying over and over, "I can't believe you didn't tell me."

I grabbed her by the shoulders. "Calm down. I just found out myself. We're interrogating the guy right now. Put the groceries away and I'll be back in a few minutes."

"Don't you leave me out here alone."

"I'll send Seeker out."

I went back into the private room and sent Seeker to stay with Sissy while we took the guy out for a beating. We busted his nose, mouth, blackened an eye, and kicked him enough times while he was on the ground to break his ribs. Old Man and Dough Boy tossed him in the van and then dumped him off downtown where his buddies could find him.

We had to send a message and we hoped that message was loud and clear: *If you want me, come get me.*

That kind of behavior wasn't new to us. It seemed like every couple of days we roughed up someone. We played the badass to the hilt. That's what made being undercover so tough. Our hearts felt one way, but we had to act another. At times it wasn't easy. But we had to do what we had to do. We did or we'd get killed. It certainly was a juxtaposed life, living and acting like a biker while dying daily in Christ.

It just never seemed to stop. And since we didn't patch, it seemed to get worse.

My birthday was coming up soon and Sissy wanted to take me away for a quiet weekend. Thank God we sold the bar so we didn't have that to worry about any longer. She was about to book our reservations when Willy announced that he was about to turn forty. And he'd never had a birthday party. Ever. Half drunk that night at the club, he announced, "I think you chumps ought to throw me a party."

"Boss's birthday is the day after yours," said Seeker. 'Why don't we celebrate both with a *bigger* party."

Willy raised his glass and said, "I'll drink to that."

I stole a glance at Sissy who was in the kitchen within earshot. "It'll be okay," I mouthed and she looked away.

So the next weekend, Willy and I celebrated our birthdays in a combined party. The guys and property girls went all out. There were balloons all over the inside of the clubhouse, some inappropriate for little kids (and thank goodness none were invited), two cakes—one for each of us—with joints for the candles and lots and lots and lots of booze. The party started with a rousing rendition of the birthday song while the two of us wore silly cardboard party hats.

Smitty rolled up during the middle of the afternoon. I didn't expect him, but was glad he came by. I met him at his bike before he could slide off. He wore a huge grin that concerned me. Something was up.

"Why the grin? You bring some new strippers?"

"Better," he said while getting off his bike. He pulled something from his saddlebag and handed it to me. "Happy birthday."

"Patches? Today?"

"What better day than your birthday celebration?"

"What about Tiger?"

"You leave that old fart to me. We're patching you guys today."

Not everyone knows when they'll be patched. The day usually begins with the probates on guard duty at the gate while everyone else parties. At some point, a patched brother will walk up to one of the probates and order him to build a bonfire. While the probate builds the fire, a different patch will wander over and ask why the guy isn't on the gate and will order him back. Then the first brother will see the probate at the gate and order him to finish the building the fire. The two patched brothers take turns running the guy ragged because, like in the military, you can't say anything. You simply follow your last order. When the

130

patches are done having fun, one of them will hit the probate while he's either at the bonfire or the gate and say, "Does the club owe you?"

The reply from the probate must be, "No sir, I owe everything to the club."

The patches then beat the tar out of the probate, sometimes to the point that when he earns the patch, he can barely hold the sewing kit to put on his patch.

We patched a little different that night. I fully expected to knuckle up with Smitty, but that didn't happen. I got off easy and I'm not sure why. Still, I shook so bad that I could barely sew on my patch.

The rest of my guys got beat on, though, and by the end of the night we were patched, something guys had waited weeks for. The celebration went up a notch after we patched. More booze. More weed. More smiles. My boys were excited to finally be a "real" bike club, The Forsaken Ones. But I had one more piece of business to take care of. I called Smitty away from the fire the boys had built and took him inside the clubhouse.

I think he saw the concern on my face. "What's up, Boss? You don't look like you're in a celebrating mood," He patted me on the shoulder as we took our seats at the bar. "I think you'd be happy as a lark right now."

I forced a grin. "I am, but I've got something I need to tell you."

"You know me, don't beat around the bush. Come right out with it."

"There's a hit on you."

He didn't even flinch, like he'd heard that a thousand times before. But he didn't say anything for the longest time. We sat staring at each other. I think he was searching my face to see if this was a lie or if I was joking around. "Well, ain't that the crapper. To find out tonight, of all nights."

"I'm sorry. I couldn't keep it inside any longer."

He patted me on the shoulder again. "Nothing to be sorry about. You're just looking out for me. No sense getting down about it." He paused and looked away, his gaze growing distant. "Who?"

"Tiger."

"I figured." He looked back at me. "When did you find out?"

"Day before last."

"How much longer did you plan to wait to tell me?"

"If you didn't show up today, I planned to ride out to your place tomorrow and tell you."

"Why?"

"Because I couldn't tell you before then."

"No, dummy. Why is the hit on me?"

"I assume it's Tiger systematically getting rid of the old guard. That's been the rumor and now it seems he's putting the wheels in motion."

Smitty stood with a determined look on his face.

"Where you going?" I stood too.

132

"Home. To figure out how I plan to take that idiot down."

Chapter 10

Which Came First...The Rain, a Taco, or a Kilo?

A week after we got patched, Red stopped by the clubhouse one morning to discuss a deal he wanted us to make with the cartel. Our first deal had gone well so the Feds wanted another. We bought two kilos from them and the deal lasted about ten minutes, although the intensity was off the charts. I hadn't experienced anything like that in my life. Inside, I shook like a naked man standing in the middle of a frozen lake, but I kept praying that God would keep us safe and me calm enough on the outside to make the exchange. When I took the dope from the contact, my hand didn't shake one iota.

Red and I left in the van to get a bite at the diner where we frequently met. Nicole, our regular waitress, was on duty and seated us right away despite the line out the door for the lunch rush.

"Whattaya you boys have today?" she asked in a singsong voice.

While we placed our orders, him a diet coke and me a water, I noticed she stood a little closer to Red than normal. She left to get our drinks and I asked, "What's the deal with that?"

"With what?" he answered while glancing out the window.

"Ah ha, you hooked up with her, didn't you?"

Still looking out the window, he said. "That obvious, huh?"

"I had it pegged the first time we came in here."

"Seriously? Even then?" he looked back at me and smiled.

"Any way," I started to say something but she returned with our drinks and to take our order. This time she stood in her normal spot at the edge of the table.

When she left, Red looked hurt. "Well, that was different."

"Cut it out, it's nothing. What do you expect? For her to sit in your lap while she takes your order? Seriously, man. She's just being professional so she doesn't lose her job."

From where we sat in the back, Red could watch her every move. And he did. We chitchatted until she brought our food to the table. She set the double cheeseburger and fries in front of him and then my lunch special of fried fish and fries with a side of celery in front of me.

Before she walked away, he asked, "Tonight?"

She paused, gave him a sheepish grin as a hint of pink emerged on her cheeks. "Same time and place?"

"Of course."

I rolled my eyes. She walked, or rather, *sashayed* away, and I asked, "Feel better now?"

"Much," he said, right before taking a huge bite of his burger.

We talked about stuff in between bites. Nicole made a number of unnecessary trips to the table. It seemed every time he took a drink, she was back the table to top him off.

As she cleared our plates, I said to her, "We need some time to talk in private."

She seemed to get the hint because Red waved in her direction three times before she noticed that he was trying to get her attention. I couldn't fault Red for being attracted to her. Since she got to know us, her perky attitude matched her perky little body. She wore her long black hair in a ponytail that she pulled over her left shoulder. She often twirled the end while talking with us.

We both felt comfortable with her, and obviously Red a little more than me. Well, a lot more than me. For me to know her the way he did, I would have to cheat on Sissy. No one on this planet, not even a parade of supermodels, could cause an urge for me to break my vows.

We talked for an hour about the club dealings, what happened at my birthday party, and our thoughts on the new Harley while the lunch crowd thinned out.

Sissy called and interrupted the conversation. She seemed upset and disgusted. "I just got off the phone with Big Brian. He asked me to open a brothel. Again. I told him that I didn't have any interest and neither did you. He kept pushing and I finally said to him that I would call you."

136

"You know we don't want to do that."

"I know, but he won't take no for an answer." I could hear the frustration in her voice. "This is the third time he's called me in the last two weeks. He keeps saying that I am just the girl for the job because all the property girls respect and trust me. I need you to call him back and tell him that we're not interested."

"I'm with Red right now. I'll call Big Brian after we finish."

"Please do. I don't feel like talking to him about it again."

I hung up with Sissy and explained the situation to a curious Red.

"Why don't you want to run a brothel? We can line up the girls with no problem."

"I know. That's not the problem. I know where the girls are from. That bothers me."

If there was a job to be done, Red, Sissy and I could make it happen. That was never an issue. We are doers. The issue is in mine and Sissy's hearts. We knew there was a line and we promised ourselves we would never cross it. Letting a woman think that the only way to gain love or respect was to sell her body to someone for the club's gain was not an option, much less recruiting or kidnapping young girls against their wills and expecting such things out of them.

He furrowed his brow.

"C'mon, you know where they get those girls." I said.

"I do, but I want to see if you do."

Anger flushed through my face and shoulders. "They snatch

those girls from school, homes, playgrounds. You name it. I want no part of that. If I had a daughter and she got snatched up it would be a bad day for whoever did it."

"Some of the girls go in willingly."

I folded my hands on the table to help hide my anger. "Not many, and if they do it's because they are looking for something that is missing in their life, love, acceptance, a family. "

We sat in silence for a few minutes until Red spoke up. "Then don't do it. Tell Big Brian that you and Sissy aren't up for running another business at the moment. Tell him you need to recover. That'll buy you some time."

"What then?"

"He'll find someone else to run it."

"What about the girls he'll use?"

"Sex trafficking will add another layer to the case."

I frowned. "In the meantime, the girls get used up. I can't let that happen. I need to keep him from opening a brothel."

"Convince him there's no money in it and he'll move on from it."

"That I can do." I unclasped my hands and silently asked the Lord for the strength and the words to say when I had to make that call. "Now, did you really bring me here to talk about the cartel or was that a ruse to get down here to make a date with your little play toy over there?" I nodded my head in her direction.

He looked toward her and they exchanged a wanton stare.

I stood to leave.

"Sit down and we'll talk."

"Switch seats with me so you can't see her."

Red reluctantly took my spot and I took his.

"Happy?" he said.

"Talk. My butt is getting sore from sitting on this cheap vinyl."

For the next half hour, he mapped out a well-planned deal with the cartel that would lay the groundwork to send a lot of people up the river for a long, long time. *This was the granddaddy*, he said. The one we needed to wrap this up soon. I sighed, hoping he was right. I didn't see any holes in his plan. Whoever came up with it certainly thought it through. This seemed like an easy deal that we could pull off with little or no effort. Boy, was I wrong.

On the ride back to the club, I called my contact at the cartel to set up the deal, scheduled for a week from today. He kept talking in Spanish even as I said repeatedly, "English, man, English."

I think he kept talking in Spanish to either piss me off or to show me who was in charge. I let him think that he was in charge. Because he didn't know that talking with two Feds was eventually going to send him and his boys to jail for a long, long time. While I struggled with doing that to my boys, I had no problem with this guy. So I put him on speaker so Red could translate for me. The contact continued to talk in Spanish so I allowed Red to finalize the plans for the deal. They talked for a few minutes and after they hung up, Red filled me in with what was about to go down.

We were to meet at a taco stand that the guys in the club had visited numerous times over the last few weeks after Dough Boy got pissed off at the location near the clubhouse and found this new one. The place literally was a little shack with an awning over a fifteen by twenty concrete slab. A depleted warehouse with boards over the windows and doors stood behind the taco stand. I had my suspicions about the place. Now I knew.

Everything seemed in place when we got back to the clubhouse. We just needed the cash from the Feds to buy seven kilos of coke. I called Ramey before we got out of the van. "You'll have it in five days," he said.

I had mixed emotions as exited the van. Those who have never been involved in a drug deal have no idea the adrenaline that courses through you during a deal. All your senses are on high alert. We lived for the rush while in the military and that's probably why many of us get into stuff like selling dope when we get back on U.S. soil. Yes, the deal can be scary on one hand, particularly if dealing with someone with the reputation of the cartel or other motorcycle gangs. They'll kill you and not even think twice about it. That's why when guys get busted, the murder charges are extensive.

As I walked up the stairs and into the club all I could think about was how we had got to here. The cartel. Dealing drugs with the actual cartel. About that time Seeker came flying out the doors to the bar.

"Boss, something is going on with your old lady."

Confused I asked, "What do you mean something is wrong? Where is she?"

"Sitting at the bar drinking whiskey. Shot for shot with Goat." He said with a surprised tone.

I knew that this could not be good because if Sissy was drinking whiskey it meant she had something heavy on her mind and that was her way of trying to forget whatever it may be.

"Hey babe. What you got there? A little cocktail, I see." I said with a smile, trying to make light of whatever was on her mind.

"Don't." She said putting her hand up with an expressionless face.

"Well Goat, I'll have what she is havin'." Goat whirled around on his stool, grabbed the bottle of whiskey and poured some in a shot glass.

"One for you and one… Oops!" He missed his own shot glass and poured the whiskey all over the bar.

"Boss, I think I am done for the night. Is that ok?" He slurred.

"I think so too, Goat. Give me your key and get to bed." I ordered.

Goat dug in his pocket and handed me the keys to his bike and stumbled to the couch in the front room.

"Seeker says you have been drinking shot for shot with Goat.

141

How are you still sitting on that stool?" I asked Sissy as she sat next to me, staring at the calendar that hung behind the bar.

She slid a red plastic cup in my direction that was filled with whiskey. "I was pouring most of them in here." She grumbled. "I just wanted one, and you know how Goat is when it comes to whiskey."

" Ah, You are a smart lady, you know that?' I leaned in for a peck on the cheek and Sissy turned away.

"What is your deal?" I asked with irritation.

" Really Boss? Really? I bet you haven't even called Big Brian yet, have you?"

I knew that this was not going to be a good conversation and so I grabbed Sissy's hand and escorted her into the private room, touching the flag as I walked in as usual and closing the door behind us.

"Do you have any idea what it is like to see these women do what they do for this club? I see it!" She sobbed.

"I watch these men take advantage of them by getting them drunk and whatever else and making them strip and sleep with every Tom, Dick or Harry so they can make money." She rambled.

"And these other poor girls that the guys bring in, we know that most of them are not even legal age and some not even willing participants. Most days after a night of sleeping with sleazy men and stripping, the girls will wake up asking anyone and everyone, "what happened?" or, "how did I get there?" All the guys do is just give her a Bloody Mary and tell her to shut up, get on the back of their bike and

142

take her to the next club." Sissy ranted with sarcasm and anger in her voice. "Like it's nothing! Another day, another dollar."

I tried to calm her down. "Sissy, listen."

"Don't tell me to listen. You get on the phone and call Big Brian and whoever else you need to call and tell them that it is not an option and to not bring it to this house!" she demanded as she glared at me with her nose almost touching mine.

I know where Sissy was coming from and I could not get upset with her compassion for the issue. I had to think of a way to tell Big Brian without telling him, "Because my old lady said so," or that I didn't agree with it. That would never fly with any of the guys and could blow my cover.

I reassured Sissy that I would handle it. She didn't seem convinced but said she would let it go for the night. This was good because I still had so much more to deal with before the night was over. Sissy grabbed her laptop and plopped down on the couch, "I am just going to stay here and rest while you go finish up with Red. Can you ask Seeker to tell the girls I just want some alone time please?"

"I can do that." I leaned down to kiss her on the cheek and this time she let me. She threw her arms around my neck and squeezed.

"I thank God for you every day." She whispered.

"I'm sorry I get so upset. I just want it to be over. I know that I have to trust in Him and know that we are in this storm for a reason. I just wish I knew why." She sniffed, wiped her own tears and went back to looking at her computer.

I walked out of the room and closed the door behind me and thought to myself that Sissy was right. We do have to trust in God and that this is all part of His plan.

Before Red left that day he told me to round up some guys for guard duty on the deal for $100 apiece. That's not a lot of money to put your life on the line. One hundred bucks. I spread the word and five guys jumped at the opportunity. The guys also didn't know that for one hundred bucks, the Feds would be gathering enough evidence to put them away for fifteen to twenty-five years. They didn't know that, but Sissy and I did. For that reason, I declined Seeker's plea for guard duty that night. Although he jumped to my rescue with the motor mouth a few weeks back, I couldn't put him in harm's way when he was so close to finding the truth on his own.

He was disappointed that I wouldn't let him ride with us, but after a long talk he understood, at least I think he did, why it was best for him to stay at the clubhouse and keep things under control there. From my experience, if things went bad at the deal, the cartel might have planned a hit on the club too. I explained to Seeker that I not only needed good people at the deal, but also at the clubhouse in case that happened.

I also didn't want Sissy at the club that night for that reason. She wouldn't have it. Letting her stay at the club actually was a compromise because she wanted to come with us.

144

"Absolutely not," I said, when the conversation came up at home a few days before the deal.

"I'm going," she said. "I'm not letting you go by yourself."

"Willy, Chief, Badger, and Goat will be with me."

"I don't care." She stood in the kitchen with her hands on her hips. "I'm going."

"You'll only be in the way."

"No, I won't. I'll stay on the bike.

"You're not going." I paced. "These guys are ex-military. They know how to handle a situation if it gets intense or starts to get out of control." I stopped and looked at her. "What would you do? Hide behind the bike?" I paced again, from the kitchen into the adjoining dining room and back. "You're not going."

"What if you get shot? Who will take care of you?"

I started to understand her thoughts, but there was no way I could let her go with us on the deal. No way. At all. "If I get shot, everyone will probably get shot, including you if you're with us."

"I want to go. I have a bad feeling about this one."

"Everything will be fine," I said, although I didn't know that for sure. We could roll up and all get gunned down before we even got off our bikes and the cartel could take our dope without paying.

I took her in my arms and said, "The best thing you can do is stay here or at the clubhouse and pray that all goes well. If you go with us, you could get hurt."

"So you're expecting to get hurt."

"I didn't say that. I said you could get hurt. With the understanding that if something went down." Then I added, "You can't defend yourself."

"I know how to shoot. Better than you."

I laughed, remembering the time we went to a shooting range while we dated. Sissy did outshoot me. She brought a pistol that she owned and one I wasn't familiar with. "You got lucky that day. That wouldn't happen again."

After a long, long discussion, I finally got her to agree to stay at the clubhouse with Dick, Seeker, Old Man, and three property girls—Squaw, Jersey, and Pippie. Squaw was dating Chief and Jersey was Goat's old lady. We'd gotten close to Squaw. She was a huge support for Sissy. Jersey, on the other hand, was usually sweet to others, but for some reason didn't get along with Sissy. We found out right before we got pulled out that Jersey thought Sissy had the hots for her old man. That certainly was the furthest thing from the truth. When Jersey found that out, she apologized for being a snot to Sissy. Sissy and I didn't care much for Pippie because she slept with most of the guys in our club and just about anyone who visited from another club. She dated Badger, and I don't know how he put up with it. I don't ever recall him stepping out on her.

So, I felt like we were all set. Until that night. A driving rain swept into the area about 4:00 p.m. that wouldn't let up. Instead of riding our bikes to the deal, we all piled into the van. Sissy walked outside with me and protested again. "Please," she begged with her voice and eyes, "let me go."

"I can't."

"What if you drive up into a trap and they just gun you guys down before you can get out of the van?"

"That's not going to happen." And again, I didn't know if that was true.

"I told you that I don't have a good feeling about this."

Red blew the horn. "So pray extra hard. And promise you'll stay here."

Some of the streets had started to flood and Red had to ease through two spots that I wasn't sure we could get though. This put us a little behind and I was beginning to worry if we would arrive on time. During the drive, we went over the details one last time. Red was to handle the exchange of the money while Willy stood guard over him. Chief, Badger, Goat and me were to stay in the van while Goat kept an AK-47 trained on the contact from the cartel.

I still couldn't believe that we planned this deal at this location, right in the middle of town. I was shocked to learn the cartel was dealing drugs right under the noses of the local police. *Someone must be on the take*, I thought.

Red pulled into the parking lot two minutes early. I sighed. You never want to be late for a deal. When you're late, the other person immediately thinks you're working with the cops. We were, but they didn't know that.

We loved the authentic tacos served here. They were much better than the cheap ones you get at a Tex-Mex place. Red left the van idling, and he and Willy got out. Willy carried his preferred weapon, an Intratec TEC-DC9 with a thirty-two-round magazine. This semi-automatic pistol contained two features listed in the Federal Assault Weapons Ban—a threaded barrel and a magazine that attaches outside the pistol grip. Having a banned weapon wasn't a big deal to us. Only law-abiding citizens worry about bans. Crooks always get their hands on whatever they want.

Red and Willy sloshed through the rain to the covering of the awning. Our headlights cast a pale glow over the patio. One wooden picnic table that had seen better days sat in the middle, perpendicular to us. Normally eight or ten tables were crammed together. Red sat on the bench to the right. Willy stood behind him and off to the side a little so he could keep his eyes on the warehouse.

Our cartel contact stepped from the little door next to the window where patrons placed their orders. Red stood and they shook hands.

I couldn't take it sitting in the van, so I slid the side door open and got out in the rain.

"What the hell are you doing?" Badger said. "Get back in here."

"I'm fine out here," I said, pulling the hood of my raincoat over my head. "I feel like I'm cooped up in a cage sitting in there with you stinkholes." They laughed at the comment. I slid the door shut and then leaned against the passenger door. I could hear people moving in and out of the warehouse.

In a quick motion, Red half-turned, while keeping his eyes on the contact, and said something to Willy, who took a step closer and chambered a round. Red returned his focus to the contact and continued the conversation in Spanish.

This didn't look good. *Dang, I wish I could carry a gun,* I thought. Goat, who had moved into the passenger's seat, said something and I told him to shut up. I wanted to hear what was going on, even though I didn't understand Spanish.

A moment later, the guy from the cartel left the table and went back inside the taco stand. Red and Willy didn't move. I could feel a nervous twitch in my legs, a tingling that I get when something isn't right. *Sissy might be right about this going all wrong in a hurry.* I said a silent prayer for protection, as the tingling grew stronger.

The hard rain continued but I still could hear warehouse doors opening and closing. Red and Willy remained still. A non-military person might have had a hard time holding their position in a situation such as this. But we're trained to hold our spot and our position for hours, if need be.

Goat tried to say something again, and I turned to him and said. "Would you please just shut the hell up?"

Before he could respond, our contact stepped out of the taco

149

stand with two guys following him. Big guys, too. The size of guys you see portrayed in movies for deals like this. One of their faces was covered in tattoos like Mike Tyson.

The contact sat across from Red again and said a few words while the other two guys stood guard over them. I couldn't see a gun on either of their hips, but they had to be packing for sure. Red pulled a large manila envelope from inside his cut and slid it across the table. The envelope contained $133,000. That's more money than most people make in a year. And that much money didn't mean a thing to us. We'd cut the dope and make three times that much on the street.

The contact pulled one of the thirteen wads of $10,000 and thumbed the edge. He smiled and then checked the other twelve, as well as the short bundle of $3,000. He nodded, and said something to his guys without taking his gaze off Red.

His brutes left and returned a few minutes later with the dope. Red said something and one of the guys put a bag on the table. Red cut it open, stuck his finger in the bag, and tasted it. He nodded, stood, and backed away from the table. One thing you learn about a deal, you don't want to turn your back on the guy you're dealing with. That's a good way to get shot. Red waited for the guy to come around the table and they walked shoulder to shoulder to the back of the van with the guards close behind. Willy followed them.

Before they got within earshot, I said to Goat, "On 'em when Red opens the back of the van."

Goat scrambled from the passenger seat to the back just as Red opened the doors. The cartel guards laid the kilos in a line just inside the doors. After they placed the dope in the back and returned to the patio, I opened the side door and caught a glimpse of something shiny near a tree about 100 yards away from the taco stand. At first, I thought it was a gun, but then realized that it must have been a Fed taking pictures of the deal. I got in and Red backed out, leaving the three cartel members standing on the patio watching us.

On the drive back to the clubhouse, Red decided he wanted to celebrate in style. He pulled into a liquor store, and after parking, he pulled $300 from his pocket and handed it to me. "Buy as much as you can. We have a lot to celebrate."

While I was inside, he paid the four their cut of guard duty. I still scratch my head over that one. One hundred bucks for so little.

While in the liquor store, Sissy called. Again. I had felt my phone vibrate numerous times while the deal was going down, but I couldn't answer it. I snapped open the phone.

"Thank God you're still alive." I could hear the relief in her voice. "Why haven't you been answering your phone?"

"I couldn't. But I'm okay and we'll be back in a few minutes."

"Hurry." Her voiced cracked.

Sissy stood on the porch out of the rain waiting for us to roll through the gate. Before Red came to a complete stop, she was off the porch. She pulled open the side door as Red put the can in "park." She

151

jumped on me, wrapped her arms around me and buried her face between my neck and shoulder. She didn't say a word or make a sound. She simply sobbed. Hard.

"Okay, that's enough," Badger said. "Some of us would like to get out of the van now."

The guys were pretty pumped up when we got back. They felt like we'd landed in the big time with our second dope deal with the cartel. We sat around the bar doing shots. After one of his shots, Goat asked, "Okay, Boss, can we do that again soon?"

"I dunno," I said. "When do you want to do the next one?"

"Tomorrow." He laughed and ordered another shot. "That was some intense shit out there tonight." He downed his shot. "But next time I want to guard Red."

"You couldn't handle it," Willy chimed in. "You'd end up shooting him in the foot."

Goat, with Jersey on his lap, heaved his shot glass at Willy, who caught it.

"When you can throw harder, you can guard the man making the exchange."

Goat threw another shot glass and Willy caught that one too.

A little while later Red rose to leave. "Great job tonight, boys. Well done."

I walked with him to his bike. "We get what we need?"

He nodded, smiling. "I think so."

152

"You meeting Nicole?"

His smile widened.

"Well, don't do anything that I wouldn't."

"I do all the time." He fired up his bike and rolled out.

And I stood there hoping Red was right—that we got what we needed. With a hit on me, I knew we wouldn't have too many more chances if tonight wasn't enough.

Chapter 11
A Shotgun, a Nine, and a Purpose

Things started to get out of hand after the drug deal with the cartel. We certainly weren't little choirboys before. If we rolled up on some place to get a bite to eat, and a "weekend warrior" as we called them, was on a bike in a spot that we wanted, we thought nothing of forcing him to roll his bike out backwards and take his spot. And we didn't just make him back out, we'd slap him on the head and punch him while he moved his bike out of the way for us. And that was on a day of good behavior.

We didn't always pull a gun or knife on someone, but we made sure they were visible, more for intimidation than anything. Usually that was enough. Sometimes I felt like we lived in the lawless old west of Tombstone, or some place like that. One of the worst nights began when we stopped for some tacos at the place where the cartel deal went down. While I was at the window placing my order, the guy with the face tattoo entered through a door at the back of the taco stand. He said something in Spanish to the woman making tacos and left. When I got my plate, I had an extra taco that I hadn't ordered. I took this as a sign that our contact was happy with the dope we sold them. That was good news because Ramey and Hector wanted us to set up another deal.

I chowed down my three tacos and drank a beer while hamming it up with Sissy, Dough Boy, Old Man, Badger, Jersey, Chief, Squaw, and Goat. Jersey is Goats old lady, who was running solo that night. After I'd finished, Sissy nudged me and nodded toward my plate. Scribbled in English was a date and location for the next deal. *That'll make Ramey happy*, I thought. I looked up and the tattoo guy stood at the far corner. I nodded, and he disappeared behind that taco stand, presumably to do something in the warehouse.

During dinner, Goat suggested we check out our old bar. Sissy and I had no desire. Too many memories, we said. But the guys talked us into it. We walked in and were promptly greeted by the new owner, a nice fellow who we felt comfortable selling the place to.

"Hey, man," I said. "We're not looking to cause trouble. We just wanted to stop by for a few drinks and support you."

"As long as there's no trouble, you can stay," he said, eyeing the guys behind me. "The first sign of trouble, I'll ask you to leave."

"Not a problem." I looked at Badger. "You got that?"

"Not a problem," he said, smiling.

Sissy and I split off from the rest of the guys and sat at the end of the bar. We struggled more and more each day to find some alone time. Some days we got just ten minutes. Being undercover was causing a huge problem in our marriage. Sissy didn't have anyone to talk with about was what going on, only Squaw really. By this point we were celebrating everything—birthday and all holidays—at the clubhouse. We just didn't have any down time. And for me, the line was getting blurred between club and family. We also knew the friends we made weren't lifelong friends. The friendships were real, but they wouldn't last. All humans need companionship and friendship, and we knew this was temporary. Smitty told me one day that I needed to get out. He could see that Sissy and I loved each other and that the club was hurting our marriage. "It's not worth it," he said.

So, we sat at the end of the bar where we'd had numerous conversations during the time we owned this place. I ordered a beer and Sissy ordered a margarita. The new owner came down to our end and we chatted about the difficulties of owning the bar. Like us, he attracted a big crowd each night for the first couple of weeks but the crowds were already declining. We told him that we tried setting up a dart league and trivia night. Neither took hold. He wanted to try karaoke or drinking contests on the weekends. Like us, the initial thought was to cater to the upper middle class clientele. And like us, I got the impression he knew that group couldn't sustain his business.

While drinking my third beer, Goat, Badger, and Chief came over to tell us they were going for a ride. I can't say that I blamed them. Nighttime rides are some of the best.

"What about your old ladies?" I said to Goat and Badger.

"Old Man and Dough Boy are taking 'em," said Chief.

I shrugged. "Well, just keep 'em between the lines boys."

They took off and Sissy and I stayed until closing time. Jersey and Squaw left with Dough Boy and Old Man about an hour before closing. My phone started blowing up right before we left. I ignored it until we walked outside to leave. Badger had sent about ten messages asking us to meet them at the clubhouse. *Important*, he said. Then it was, *very important*. The last one: *You gotta get here soon.*

An animated Chief and Badger were on the front porch when we rolled through the gate. At first I thought they were about to have it out. I shut off the bike and, before getting off, asked, "What's going on, boys?"

"You are not going to believe this," Badger said. "We just jacked up some guy."

"What guy?" I suddenly grew concerned.

Badger bounced up and down like a little kid all sugared up. "At the bar we heard about this guy who beat up his old lady."

"I'm listening," I said, reaching inside my cut to turn on my recorder. This can't be good, I thought.

"Tell him, Chief."

Chief, grinning as wide as I had ever seen him, took over. "At the bar, this couple in the booth behind us was talking about some guy who beat up his old lady. The guy broke her nose and a couple of ribs. I can't stand that, man. My old man used to beat my mom. I hated him for that. So all that came rushing back and I wanted to do something. I

157

started to get up but Badger held me back and we listened some more. The woman was pretty upset because she knew the gal who got beat up. I couldn't take it anymore so I got up and slid into their booth. You should have seen the look on their faces." He chuckled. "I asked where the woman lived. The one in the booth blurted out the address before the guy could stop her. I thanked them and that's when we came over to tell you that we were leaving."

"Please tell me that you didn't kill the guy."

"Oh no," Badger said. "But I bet he wishes we had."

"What," I tried to keep my voice even, "did you do to him?" I noticed Sissy standing next to me for the first time since Chief and Badger started telling the story.

Chief picked up the story again. "So we roll up to this place and knocked on the door. Nice house. Upscale two-story place with pillars."

"Enough with the description," Badger said. "Tell the story."

"Okay, okay," Chief said. "So the guy answered the door and I dropped him. I was about to kick him when the woman came around the corner. She looked bad. Real bad. This guy did a real number on her. I wanted to kick him harder now. She didn't even scream. She just said, 'That's not him. That's my brother. He's here to protect me.'

"I felt bad for punching the guy and reached down to help him up. He swatted my hand away and scooted farther into the house. Badger then asked the woman where the guy was and she told us at his mother's and gave us the address. We turned to leave and she said, 'Please, don't kill him.' I promised that we wouldn't. But deep down, I wanted to.

"So we get to this guy's mother's house and this time Goat knocked on the door."

"Where is Goat?" I asked.

"Inside, passed out," Chief said. "So after Goat knocked, the guy answered and Goat dropped him. He went down hard. I could see a patio at the back of the house, so I grabbed him by the collar and started dragging him through the house. I'm jacked up at this point and really wanted to beat on this guy. We passed the kitchen, I noticed a bag of kitty litter on the floor and I grabbed it. I kicked open the door and flung the guy outside.

"Chief tied the guy's hands behind his back and slammed the bag of kitty litter on his head. He tried to spit it out but I kept pounding on his head until he stopped."

I shook my head. *This was gonna be bad*, I could tell. Chief and Badger were too fired up not to have done something stupid. "Where was this again?"

Chief repeated the address and continued, "Let me tell you, we beat the hell out of that guy. We took turns punching the guy in the head and gut while the other two held him up. When I took my second turn I grabbed a bag of fertilizer that was next to some potted flowers and started beating him in the face with it. The kitty litter bag broke, and then the fertilizer bag broke. Badger and Goat let him go and he fell into the pile of fertilizer. I stomped his head in it while Badger and Goat

159

kicked him until he quit making any noises. I thought we might have killed him, but I felt his pulse and then we left."

Chief started bouncing again after being serious while describing the attack. "It was awesome. We beat that guy senseless. He'll think twice about beating on a woman again."

Badger added, "He's busted up pretty bad. I heard some bones break." He lifted a boot and pointed it at me. "These babies right here did some serious damage."

"Well, boys, sounds like you had a great night." I said, catching the look on Sissy's face. She seemed shocked and distressed. "You gonna hang out here?"

They replied in unison that they were.

"Sissy and I are gonna stay at our house tonight. You boys have a good one." And then we took off. I couldn't get away fast enough and spun the tires a little bit. Halfway home I pulled over to call Ramey. "You better get the cops and an ambulance over to this address right away. My boys just beat the tar out of someone and he might be dead."

I know being a biker means doing crazy shit. But that night I thought that would be the worst. But it wasn't. I saw something a few weeks later that, although no one got hurt, certainly took the cake.

In less than a week, two of my buddies got killed in motorcycle accidents. I was really close with the second guy, Barry. He died one morning when he ran into the side of a garbage truck on the way to his clubhouse. Smacked it at full speed. Why, no one knows. He didn't seem like the kind of guy who would commit suicide. I was tore up when I got the news. I spent most of the day crying. I didn't stay at the clubhouse that day. I needed to be away from the guys so I could cry and pray without prying eyes.

Ramey and Hector must have heard about Barry's death the same day because the calls started right away. I knew what they wanted, to know the date and location of the funeral. I didn't have it for a few days and they both got upset when I told them I didn't know. But I didn't.

I found out the day before the funeral and called Ramey, who got a little testy with me saying, "We need more time, you know that."

"I do know that," I shot back. "But I literally found out an hour ago."

Losing a brother is a big deal. A real big deal. When Joe CEO of a local business loses a loved one, he'll be at a loss for a while but as the years pass, more than likely he'll visit the gravesite less and less. Bikers, on the other hand, never forget. Ever. Each year on the anniversary of a fallen brother, we honor them with a ride. Everyone rides, even new members and probates that have joined in the year since the brother passed away.

Barry's funeral was held in his hometown, which was smack dab in the middle of enemy territory. So, of course, we called the enemy ahead of time and let them know we'd be rolling through town. Sure enough, they stood outside the fence of their clubhouse when we rolled by. We didn't acknowledge each other but you don't have to.

I met Barry's parents for the first time when we got to the church. Understandably, they were pretty shook up. I can't imagine how hard it is to bury a child, no matter how old they are. Barry was in his mid-forties at the time. We pulled up to the church and, weak from grief, I could barely stand. I don't remember what the pastor said that day. Sissy said later he spoke highly of Barry, which meant a lot to me, and I'm sure to his parents as well. I think the non-bikers in attendance were quite shocked to see us crying, especially me. I hadn't cried like that in a long, long time. I was pretty choked up by the time we left the church.

We led the procession to the cemetery where we discovered the Feds hanging from the trees in harnesses. I wanted to puke. Sometimes you see things in life and feel like there is no justice. This was one of them. We couldn't even grieve in peace for the loss of a brother. The Feds really made no attempt to hide. Along with the guys in the trees, others set up behind headstones with long telephoto lenses. That upset me because instead of paying our respect to Barry and his family, a large number of the bikers put on a show for the cameras by making faces and flipping them off.

That's just what the Feds needed, though. Ramey called the next day excited about all the pictures they got. He wanted to meet so I could ID the guys in the photos. I told him to kiss off and hung up on him. He kept calling for a few days and I wouldn't answer or respond to his texts.

Two days after the funeral, I sat in my rocker on the west side of the club looking at the mountains. Usually I sat here with Sissy at night.

162

Today, I needed some time alone to think about Barry and his soul. I loved that man, but never got a chance to talk with him about salvation. Someone approached. "Go away. I don't want to be bothered."

"I'm not here to bother you," the gentleman said. "I'm here to give you peace."

I laughed and turned to the part-time chaplain I recognized from another club. I lowered my sunglasses and offered him a seat next to me.

"Talk to me, preacher."

"The shades to shield your eyes from the sun or to hide your tears?"

I shrugged. "A little of both."

"I heard that you've been worried about Barry's soul." The chaplain leaned back in the chair. "I want you to know that he's okay."

I swallowed a lump in my throat. I so desperately needed to hear that.

"Barry and I talked often about salvation, quietly of course. I want you to know that he prayed the sinner's prayer with me about a year ago. And since that time he checked in with me about how to live a godly life in the biker community. He was serious about his faith. I want you to know that."

A tear slid down my cheek. And we sat there in silence for a good while. Finally he stood and patted me on the knee. "Don't get up."

"Thank you for coming by today. It means a lot to me."

He left and I thanked the Lord for shining his light into the dark world of motorcycle clubs to find my friend Barry.

The chaplain wasn't my only surprise visitor that week. Red came by three or four days after the funeral. "You need to talk with Ramey. He's not happy."

"Neither am I." I didn't make any attempt to hide the disgust I felt. "I really don't appreciate what happened at Barry's gravesite. That's despicable."

"Be that as it may," Red said. "You need to call him."

I did the next day and set up a time to meet the following day. I still wasn't happy, but I spent an hour pointing out guys in more than 200 pictures. When we finished, tired and angry, I blurted, "What more do you want from me? Nothing Sissy and I do seems good enough."

"I don't understand why you're complaining. Everything is under control."

"I'm about at the point that I don't care. I've had it up to here," I said, putting my hand in front of my forehead. Then I stormed off.

Sissy was worse than ever before. And I was about to join her. I really don't think they understood the pressure of being undercover in that role. The only people who could were guys like Red, who was undercover too. We had suspicions of another UC in the club, but we couldn't flush the guy out. It would have been nice if there was and we could have worked the case together, but the Feds obviously didn't want us pairing up.

My sour attitude continued until we decided to ride into Phoenix the following week. I hadn't been to Phoenix in a while. So we took off that day with me leading the way in the left front. I rode there unless someone with a higher rank, like Smitty or Splash, rode with us. In that case, I rode right front. Midway to Phoenix, I motioned to Willy, who was on my right, to switch places. That was unusual but I wanted the outside so Sissy could enjoy the scenery, which she couldn't see as well on the inside.

The move eventually saved my life. Just outside of Phoenix on Interstate 10, a woman going eastbound with us clipped Willy and almost sent him into me. I swerved and looked down to make sure that I had missed him. I did, but I saw my floorboard go right over top of his head.

With Willy sliding and spinning out of control, we all locked it down trying to get out of the way. The chorus of tires squealing sounded like a jetliner landing in the middle of the Interstate. Traffic was heavy at the time and by rights we should have all been run over. It truly was by God's grace that we weren't.

Dick came up out of his spin and took off after the woman. I found out later that he forced her to the side of the road, ran to the car, and shoved a pistol in her mouth. Old Man ran up to the car with a knife in his hand screaming, "You just hit my brother. If he dies, I'm gonna slit your throat!"

While this happened, I ran back to Willy and told Sissy to call Ramey. Willy laid face down on the road, motionless. I dropped to my knees, literally and figuratively. I tossed up some hurried and fervent prayers as I moved Willy's head carefully.

Nothing. He wasn't breathing. I stood and looked at Sissy, who was white. I mouthed, "He's gone." I couldn't believe my brother was gone. Just like that. Life truly does change in an instant.

People were honking their horns. Amidst the smell of burnt rubber and exhaust that filled the air, I did something only cops and fireman should do. "Shut it down," I screamed. I didn't want one more of my guys getting hit by someone rubbernecking.

I dropped to my knees again and put Willy's head in my lap. Sissy came to my side. "How long?"

"Huh?"

"How long since the wreck?"

"Three minutes."

We were getting close to permanent damage if the ambulance didn't arrive soon. Willy's face looked like raw hamburger meat.

Seeker stood over Willy screaming, "Don't you dare! Don't you die on me! You get back here, ya hear?"

Willy started gurgling. While I felt helpless as he made those awful sounds, I took it as a sign that he was trying to live. Blood started pouring from his mouth and eyes. Then gray matter oozed from his ears. I about lost it. His brain was seeping onto my hands as I held him.

The ambulance arrived a few minutes later. They loaded Willy and took off. We followed but when we arrived at the hospital the guards wouldn't let me enter because of my knife. I didn't have time to take it back to the bike so I tossed it in the trash.

I got Willy's vest after the medics cut it off to work on him. While we waited for news on Willy, Badger and me did our best to clean it. They didn't cut the patch, thankfully. I couldn't get over the amount of blood. So much blood.

The whole time Sissy and me prayed. And prayed even more. I honestly thought he would die. Thankfully, he didn't.

Willy spent a month in a coma. Doctors didn't give him much of a chance of making it, and if he did, he would have permanent brain damage. I prayed. Morning. Noon. Night.

For my brother.

God must have heard those prayers too. Because two months after his accident, we took Willy home to the clubhouse to nurse him back to full health. He couldn't be left alone so Sissy and I moved into the clubhouse full-time. About at the end of her rope, Sissy was so not happy about that.

For both of us, the end of being undercover couldn't get here soon enough. Little did we know that we had less time than we thought.

Chapter 12

Need Some Ice for That Burn?

The first week that Willy recovered in the clubhouse, Ramey called me constantly, sometimes three or four times in a two-hour period. I didn't know what he wanted. I had a few thoughts: another deal with the cartel, finding out when another biker funeral was, or some kind of other deal that we hadn't tried.

I wasn't up for any of that. I wanted to stay with Willy and nurse him back to health. He was in bad shape when we brought him home to the clubhouse. He could barely walk. And yes, he did suffer some brain damage. Thankfully, the damage didn't affect his motor skills. He could still talk, but experienced many outbursts of anger, like he didn't have the filter most people have to help keep it together if something upsets them. Holy crap, it was bad if he didn't like something. If you brought him food that he didn't like, he'd cuss up a storm until you gave him what he wanted. If you put on a television show that he hated, same thing, he cussed up a storm until you changed the channel to a show he wanted, even if you had seen it numerous times.

168

I guess Ramey got tired of me not answering and he started to bug Sissy, who was home getting redy for dinner night at the clubhouse. She wouldn't answer her "special" phone unless I was with her. She told me later that after a morning of constant calls, she finally answered.

"I need to talk with Boss," Ramey said.

"He's not here. Can I help you with something?"

"No, I need to talk with him."

"I can give him a message."

"We need to meet with him. Right away."

"Can I meet instead? He's busy taking care of Willy at the clubhouse."

"We need to discuss guy stuff. Have him contact me right away," he said and hung up.

Sissy called me right away and told me to call Ramey. I didn't want to. Willy was in the middle of a nap and I wanted to take one myself. Sissy convinced me to call Ramey. I walked outside where I could keep my eye on Willy while making the call. Ramey answered on the first ring.

"You need to get together with us," he said with an even voice. 'Today."

"I can't today. I'm watching Willy."

"You need to get away for a few minutes."

"How do you think that will look? If I leave? Huh?" When he didn't answer, I added. "I'll send Sissy."

169

"No, it has to be you."

"What part of I can't don't you understand?"

I gave Ramey credit; he was stern on this one. Usually he backed down when I said something like that. Although he pushed me hard at times and knew how to punch my buttons, I think he understood when I couldn't do certain things. This was not one of those times. "Your life depends on it."

That got my attention. I sighed. "What time and where?"

"Twenty minutes at the normal spot."

I called Sissy and asked her to come to the clubhouse to watch Willy. She wasn't happy, protesting loudly with a few choice words. I felt for her. She needed a break and returning to the clubhouse four hours early was cutting that break short.

I arrived on time for my meeting as usual, to see Ramey and Hector already there. That was different. Something must be up, I thought.

It was.

We sat at our normal spots and Ramey started the conversation. "We know about the hit on you."

Glancing at Ramey, Hector added, "We've known about it for the past three months."

I wanted to smack both of them. After beating the motor mouth a few months back, talk of the hit quieted down. I thought at that point the kid was just shooting off his mouth. I really had been burned and they knew about it.

And didn't tell me.

That wasn't cool. Sissy and I were about to crack and they left us in with the hit on me. I drew in a deep breath in an effort to calm my nerves. "Tell me what you know."

Then it dawned on me. The woman who hit Willy might have been trying to take me out. She wouldn't have known that we switched places. It seemed unlikely, but you just never know. I started to think of situations in which I had a close call. The only other one that came to mind was the night I got food poisoning at the taco stand after our third deal with the cartel.

Hector exchanged a look with Ramey. I was about to voice my displeasure when Hector said, "Another undercover heard about it at a party."

That confirmed what Sissy and I suspected: other agents were UC too. "And?"

"They know that you're a Fed so Splash put out the hit on you."

"That's what the guy said when we picked him up."

"How did they find out I was a Fed?"

"There'd been a rumor of a letter or a note that we only saw within the last month. There was a meeting in Colorado. Someone had a paper that listed Ramey as FBI and you as the UC."

I pounded my first on the table. I'm sure they saw the look of hate in my eyes. "And you're just now telling me."

171

"Easy, don't draw attention to us."

"I don't care about that. I think I'll tell everybody here what's going on. How about that?" I started to stand.

"Sit down," Ramey said in a fatherly voice. "Everything will be fine. You have nothing to worry about. Just keep on doing what you've been doing, taking care of Willy and getting ready for next weekend's party."

"Really? How am I supposed to do that?"

"Just act normal."

Despite all the inner turmoil, I was trying to hold it together. Everything that Sissy and I had worked for could all go down the drain in an instant if someone got to me. I couldn't fathom what that looked like. Would these guys take care of Sissy? Would they pull her out? Would they make her stay? Could they make her stay? They really had us over a barrel at times.

We got paid each month, not much, but something we could use. We didn't use it for us. Sissy's money went toward utilities and such at the clubhouse. We put as much of my money in the bank for when this was all over.

All over. That's what we wanted and it appeared that if they could keep me alive we were about done. A sense of relief washed away my anger. For a moment.

"I'm out. We're done. You're not putting Sissy or me in danger anymore."

"We need you to stay in, act like nothing's wrong, while we work this angle."

"What angle?"

"We want to know who typed up the letter."

"Why?" I raised my hands in protest. 'What difference does it make who wrote the letter?"

"It gives us another charge on them."

"My life is on the line for another charge. Nice." I bit my lip and stared at both of them. "What about Smitty? Does he believe I'm a Fed?"

"He didn't at first," Ramey said. "We have discovered that he was one of the first guys to see it and he didn't believe it. He thought it was a joke. For months, he kept denying it whenever someone brought it up to him."

"What made him change his mind?"

"We're not sure. The evidence must have become pretty convincing."

That hurt. Smitty and I had grown pretty close. Too hurt about knowing that Smitty knew, I changed the subject. "Why couldn't I bring Sissy today?"

"She can't know," Ramey said.

"No. I'm telling her." I shook my head. "I have to tell her." I looked at my watch. I needed to get back to the clubhouse. "Anything else? We have dinner night and I gotta get back."

"I don't have anything else," Hector. To Ramey, "Do you?" After he shook his head, Hector said to me, "You can't tell her. Just play it cool for the next few days."

"Here we go again. Just a few more days, or one more job, or one more connection. What happens if someone rolls up tonight and puts a gun to my head?"

"We'll be on call and we'll be there right away."

"Do you know how insane that sounds? If a guy has a gun on me, I can't say excuse me, I need to call my handler so he can come down and bust your butt." I got up and left. I hoped with every ounce of my being that there would be no more meetings with Hector and Ramey. I wasn't sure that I could sit through another without beating on both of them.

When I got back to the club, Sissy read my face and knew something was wrong. Even Willy noticed it. Both bugged me for a few minutes before I made an excuse to get something from the store for tonight's dinner. So I left again for a quick ride to clear my head. In my mind, I replayed the conversation with Ramey and Hector dozens of times. I kept going back to one thing: if they knew for months, why now? Why tell me tonight?

I pulled over and called Ramey. He sounded nervous when he answered and I told him that everything was okay. Well, that was a lie. Nothing was okay at this point. I pressed him on telling me today. "Let's just make it through the night," he said. That seemed odd at the time, but looking back I think he and Hector knew Music Man and Phil were coming that night to take our patches. I hung up and continued my ride.

I prayed for peace and safety for Sissy and me. Between Willy's wreck and this, I prayed more than I had in years. And I've been a praying man ever since, making a commitment to live for the Lord when I got out of prison. If I wasn't ripping it up through town, I'd had been on my knees pleading with the good Lord above.

Tired of riding, I finally headed back to the clubhouse. By the time our fenced-in yard came into sight I had a peace I didn't expect because of the circumstances. I smiled. Peace came because my God is bigger than any situation or circumstance.

With my spirit now soaring, I flipped on some Jaime Johnson and roared through the gate.

Chapter 13

A Raid? A Hit? An Apology?

Sissy and I got pulled out the next day. The Feds made their case, busting up a number of clubhouses in multiple states with a synchronized raid. A lot of print and television press was devoted to the event, which included the use of tanks and other extreme measures. Some reports showed the Feds removing signs from clubhouses, collecting items, and removing numerous boxes of evidence.

So in the end, the Feds got their show.

The arrests resulted in numerous indictments, which I can't reveal here, although they are public record now. All the cases went through. Some of the guys plead out, others cut a deal, and some went to trial. At the end of the day, this was a slam-dunk for the government. Because of my work, the Feds had everything either on recording or on video.

I haven't seen any of my boys since we were pulled out. I've heard through the grapevine that they've forgiven me. I hope so. I mentioned many times in this story how much it tore up Sissy and me to gather the evidence we did against people who became our friends. I heard a number of the guys told investigators that they have a hard time believing it was me because I was a true brother.

When we were in the club, those guys were our family and friends. Now, we don't have any friends. Just Jesus. And, yet, we can't attend church for fear of someone anywhere in the country recognizing us.

Our tough times haven't come to an end with the completion of the case. While I can't go into details, I will tell you that we make it through each day only by the grace of God.

For a while after we got pulled out, we lived in a state of paranoia. Every sound in the house caused panic. We constantly looked over our shoulders. Every car that pulled in behind us was a potential hit man. Sissy suffered from major anxiety for a long time.

Through it all, we've learned that God is not the God of good people. He's the God of the broken, of the failures, and of those who hurt.

We don't have to be perfect when we come to him. It doesn't matter how dirty, or even filthy, we just need to come.

A friend told me this one time: God doesn't put us in the fire to come through it alone. He gets in there with us.

Sissy and I have learned that first hand, in the club and now, that

177

God is with us. In everything we do.

We're excited about the future.

If you're not sure about your future, where you'll be eternally, seek the Lord. Find a friend who knows Jesus and get to know the Creator of the Universe and how much He loves you.

Both Sides of the Fence

For further information check out these websites:

traffinginamericataskforce.org

BishopOutreach.com

CPSIA information can be obtained at www.ICGtesting.com
Printed in the USA
LVOW05s1524221113

362420LV00004B/5/P